100 Places to Visit

GREAT DAYS OUT FOR ALL THE FAMILY

Produced by AA Publishing
© Automobile Association Developments Limited 2004
Maps © Automobile Association Developments Limited 2004.

This product includes mapping data licensed from Ordnance Survey® with the permission of the Controller of Her Majesty's Stationery Office.
Crown copyright. All rights reserved. Licence number 100021153
Reprinted Nov 2005, Jan 2006 and Oct 2008

Published by AA Publishing (a trading name of Automobile Association Developments Limited, whose registered office is Fanum House, Basing View, Basingstoke, Hampshire RG21 4EA; registered number 1878835)

A03920

ISBN-10: 0-7495-4044-3
ISBN-13: 978-0-7495-4044-9

A CIP catalogue record for this book is available from the British Library.

Produced for AA Publishing by *The Bridgewater Book Company*

Printed and bound by Leo Paper Group, China

ACKNOWLEDGEMENTS

t (top), b (bottom), c (centre), l (left), r (right), bg (background)

All images and illustrations belong to the Automobile Association's own library (AA WORLD TRAVEL LIBRARY) with the exception of p10r courtesy of the Eden Project.

t (top), b (bottom), c (centre), l (left), r (right), bg (background)

P Aithie 57; M Alexander 125l, 125r, 128r; S Anderson 119, 120l, 120r, 128l; A Baker 131l; P Baker 12r, 13r, 17l, 20r, 40l, 48bl, 77t, 107r; S Bates 55r; J Beazley 19bg tr, 69bg tr, 99, 102t, 102b, 111bg tr; 118l, 118r, 122l, 144; P Bennett 104l; M Birkitt 4r, 39l, 83l, 83r, 84t, 84b, 85t, 98r; E Bowness 3, 100b, 101tr, 101b; P Brown 36l; I Burgum 18tl, 54, 64l, 65l, 67l, 67c, 67r, 71l; J Carnie 127l, 127r; C Coe 86r; D Corrance 138t, 138b; D Croucher 33t, 33b, 64r; R Czaja 16b; S Day 15, 23l, 23r, 32l, 32r, 68tl, 74r, 75t, 75b, 78l, 78r, 80b, 88b, 90r, 91r, 122r, 132l, 132r, 133l, 133r; R Eames 116r; R Elliott 113r; R Fletcher 18bg tl, 31, 68bg tl, 68tc, 68r, 110bgtl; D Forss 35t, 42cl, 43b, 116l; S Gibson 126l; V Greaves 90l; M Hayward 72bl; J Henderson 69, 114, 130t; A Hopkins 70l, 98l; R Ireland 19bg tl, 68tc; N Jenkins 66b; C Jones 111, 16t, 19tr, 19cr, 22, 60, 61t, 61b, 81t, 82t, 82b; M Jourdan 17r, 19l, 26l, 26r, 27, 46tr, 52t; P Kenward 50l; S King 101tl; A Lawson 9l, 80t, 12l, 110cc, 111; C Lees 103; T Mackie 18bl, 87t, 87b; G Matthews 97c; S & O Mathews 21b, 45tr, 73, 81bl, 92bl; S McBride 35bl, 42tr, 42bl, 43t, 46c; E Meacher 28; J Miller 40r, 44b; C Molyneux 55l, 65r; M Moody 52b; J Morrison 18tc, 109; R Mort 47b, 53; R Moss 7l, 7r, 8, 18bg tc, 68bg tc, 110bg tc; R Newton 18bg tr, 19bg tc, 19br, 20l, 21t, 25, 62t, 68bg tr, 72tr, 106, 107l, 110bg tr; D Noble 39r, 44t; H Palmer 76; V Patel 108; K Paterson 4bl, 115t, 131r, 135, 141l; R Rainford 110cl; G Rowatt 110cc; P Sharp 121, 123; J Smith 136, 137r, 139t, 139b; T Souter 35br, 74l, 86l, 110cr; F Stephenson 79; R Strange 51bl; D Tarn 92t, 93; M Taylor 140, 141r; T Teegan 14t; R Tenison 9r, 10l; T Timms 58l, 96r, 97t; J Tims 2c, 47t, 51bc, 51r; M Trelawny 36r, 41b; R Turpin 50r; R Weir 130b, 134b, 142; S Whitehorne 112l, 112r, 115b, 117, 124, 129l, 129r, 134t; L Whitwam 85b, 89, 95cr, 95b; H Williams 14b, 41t, 70br; P Wilson 94t, 94b, 105l; T Woodcock 48tr; J Wyand 29b, 77b; W Voysey 5, 18r, 24, 29t, 30t, 30b, 34, 37tr, 37cl, 37bl, 37br, 38l, 49r, 49b, 59, 62b, 63, 71r, 96l; W Voysey/The Dean and Canons of Windsor 38r

Cover: tl Southwold-Tom Mackie, tc Inverewe Gardens-Jeff Beazley, tr Crathes Castle-Ronnie Weir, bl River Wye from Symonds Yat-AA, bc The Royal Pavilion, Brighton-Peter Baker, br The London Eye-Max Jourdan
Inside flap: Hadrian's Wall-Jeff Beazley
Spine: Blackpool Tower-Steve Day
Back cover: l Edinburgh Castle-Jonathan Smith, c Postbridge-Peter Baker, r Stourhead Gardens-Rich Newton, bg London Eye-Max Jourdann

Contents

Feature Spreads

THE LANGDALE PIKES IN THE LAKE DISTRICT

Introduction

Visitors to Britain, particularly those from much larger countries, are often amazed by the diversity contained within a relatively small area – landscape, architecture, customs, accents and even that indistinct quality we call 'atmosphere' can all vary greatly within the space of a half a day on the road. And, because of the lay of the land, many of these variations pop up suddenly to surprise you as you round a corner or reach the crest of a hill. Some of the most lonely and remote ranges of hills and moorland areas are, in fact, very close to our most vibrant cities, and in the middle of huge conurbations there are vast green areas of parkland.

This book brings together all the elements that make up the best of Britain, combining the famous places that absolutely should not be missed with lots of lesser-known delights. Britain is well worth exploring, and the words and pictures you will find within the following pages offer the incentive to set off – on wheels or foot.

A LOCH IN THE CAIRNGORMS   BRIGHTON PAVILION

Every part of the country has its own special appeal. The West Country has lush green hills, smugglers' bays and rocky sea cliffs. In the southeast, London's breathless pace and world-famous landmarks are the main focus – but even the capital's broad commuter belt has its own rural havens in the Sussex Downs and the wonderful orchards of the weald in Kent.

For a unique and evocative experience, roam the low marshlands and enjoy the wide skies and abundant bird life of the East Anglian shores. The great industrial cities of the Midlands and the North are hotbeds of culture and nightlife; and then there are the plunging valleys and isolated farms of Yorkshire; Northumberland's empty majestic coast; and the grandeur of Derbyshire's peaks. Over the border in Scotland there's a whole new range of landscapes: Edinburgh's dignified terraces and medieval Old Town; the high-octane energy, monumental architecture and stunning art collections of Glasgow; the breathtaking spaces of the Highlands; the romantic lochside castles, and the remote, mystical peace of the offshore islands. To the west there's Wales, where you can travel in one day from the sheer waterfalls and craggy mountains of the north, through deserted hill country or along the lovely sweeping coasts of Ceredigion and Pembrokeshire down to the busy south.

Where do you start? That's where this book can help: by directing you to the best of Britain, the familiar and the unexpected; by suggesting some exciting places to see to make the most of this island's store of treasures.

THE SNOWDON MOUNTAIN RAILWAY

Location Map
100 Places to Visit

Padstow

Cornwall

5 miles (8km) northwest of Wadebridge

Overlooking the Camel estuary, Padstow is the quintessential Cornish fishing port and well known for its seafood restaurants and famous chef son, Rick Stein. Life revolves around the harbour, from which a tight maze of narrow streets and alleys leads off. A passenger ferry runs to Rock, from where there are walks out to Pentire Head, while on the Padstow side you can walk north to Stepper Point for views along the coast. For cyclists, the Camel Trail is a scenic 26-mile (42km) traffic-free route along an old railway track partly following the estuary.

TOURIST INFORMATION CENTRE

THE RED BRICK BUILDING
NORTH QUAY
PADSTOW PL28 8AF

TEL: 01841 533449

ABOVE: A CHEERFUL RIOT OF COLOUR OUTSIDE A FLOWER SHOP ADDS TO THE CHARM OF THIS ATTRACTIVE PORT.

RIGHT: THERE ARE MANY SEAFOOD RESTAURANTS IN PADSTOW, WHERE LIFE REVOLVES AROUND THE HARBOUR.

St Ives
Cornwall
7 miles (12km) northeast of Penzance

TOURIST INFORMATION CENTRE

THE GUILDHALL
STREET-AN-POL
ST IVES
TR26 2DS
TEL: 01736 796297

St Ives is renowned for its modern art gallery and its arty fishing port, brimming with character. Other highlights are its excellent surfing and bathing beaches.

St Ives began life as a small fishing community that built its wealth on pilchards. During the 20th century, tourism, surfing and the town's reputation as a centre of art became a magnet for holidaymakers. The hub of the old fishing quarter is Downlong, a maze of tiny stepped streets and alleys off Fore Street, with curious names such as Salubrious Place and Teetotal Street.

Mediterranean light qualities and the magnificent coastal scenery have attracted artists to St Ives since the 1880s, when the first painters and sculptors were established here. They have included the potter Bernard Leach (1887–1979), the painter Ben Nicholson (1894–1982) and his sculptor wife Dame Barbara Hepworth (1903–75). Her studio and house in Barnoon Hill are now the Barbara Hepworth Museum and Sculpture Gallery, where everything is much as she left it when she died in a fire there.

ABOVE: THE TATE ST IVES GALLERY IS A
STYLISH MODERN BUILDING; IT MOUNTS
INNOVATIVE, CONTROVERSIAL EXHIBITIONS
AND HOUSES A COLLECTION OF WORKS
BY POST-WAR ARTISTS.

The Penwith Gallery and St Ives
Society of Artists Gallery showcase good
local art. An arts festival in September
offers a varied programme of music and
literature, while shopping tends naturally
towards art (painting and sculpture
galleries are dotted around), clothes
(lots of surfing gear) and gift shops.

FAR LEFT AND LEFT:
ALTHOUGH ST IVES IS
A LIVELY CENTRE FOR
ARTISTS, IT RETAINS ITS
CHARACTER AS AN OLD
FISHING PORT.

Eden Project
Cornwall
Bodelyn, near St Austell, 13 miles (20km) northeast of Truro

Unique in Britain, the Eden Project is one of the most talked-about and visited creations of the new millennium, examining our relationship with the natural world.

The project is a 37-acre (15ha) gateway into the world of plants located in a disused china-clay mine near St Austell. First conceived in 1994, the project received its first £37.5 million grant from the Millennium Commission in May 1997; in October, the nursery where Eden's plants are grown and quarantined was purchased and a year later building got underway. It took six months to clear the site of 1.8 million tonnes of soil.

Two gigantic framed structures, dubbed 'biomes', house a diverse range of wild and cultivated plants. Work has started on a third biome. Each biome contains areas representing the horticulture of a number of countries: the humid tropics biome has plants and products from Amazonia, West Africa, Malaysia and Oceania, and humidity and temperature are controlled to re-create rainforest conditions. The warm temperate biome focuses on Southern Africa, the Mediterranean and California, and has a magical array of Californian wild flowers. The grounds outside Eden make up the roofless biome – with plants from Britain's own temperate climate, including native Cornish flora.

LEFT AND ABOVE: UNUSUAL PLANTS FROM AROUND THE WORLD THRIVE IN THE EDEN PROJECT BIOMES.

EDEN PROJECT
BODELVA
ST AUSTELL
PL24 2SG
TEL: 01726 811911

Exeter

Devon

64 miles (103km) southwest of Bristol

TOURIST INFORMATION CENTRE

CIVIC CENTRE
PARIS STREET
EXETER EX1 1JJ

TEL: 01392 265700

BELOW: BLACK-AND-WHITE TIMBER-FRAMED BUILDINGS ON STEPCOTE HILL.
BOTTOM: STONE ANGEL ON THE CATHEDRAL

During World War II, Exeter was hit by a massive bombing raid that all but destroyed the historic centre. It continues as a regional and shopping hub, although the city's core is a mixture of ancient buildings, such as the Guildhall in the High Street, scattered among bland post-war redevelopments.

The best preserved streets include Southernhay, Stepcote Hill and the gracious close around the miraculously intact cathedral, which is considered the finest specimen of the decorated Gothic style in the country. It has the largest expanse of continuous vaulting in the world, as well as an ornate west façade and 13th-century misericords (carved benches).

The old quayside area is lively with places to eat, bars and craft shops, and there are boat tours and walkways.

Dartmoor National Park
Devon

The highest land in southern England, filling most of the space between Exeter and Plymouth, is a granite plateau of rugged, desolate beauty. The pony-grazed, heathery moors are speckled with the remains of Stone Age settlements and punctuated by streams and tors (jagged outcrops), such as the outstanding viewpoints of Hound Tor and Hay Tor. Walkers should be competent and adept at map reading, for, although there are signposts and painted stones as guides, it is best to buy a map from one of the visitor centres in any main town to find your way around the area.

Beneath the tors are cob-and-thatch villages such as Lustleigh and North Bovey. The verdant east side includes the Teign Valley and the dramatic Becky Falls.

The granite tors – the great rounded bosses of rock that thrust out of the moor – are favourite climbing venues. Granite is popular amongst rock-climbers because of its solidity and its generous holds. This is a serious but immensely rewarding sport and Dartmoor is an ideal place to start before attempting more difficult climbs. The top challenging climbing crags are: Screda Point at Hartland Quay; the Dewerstone, near Plymouth; Haytor, near Bovey Tracey; Combshead Tor, near Burrator Reservoir; and the Old Redoubt, Berry Head, near Brixham.

FAR LEFT: STUNTED AND GNARLED TREES GROW AMONG MOSS-COVERED ROCKS IN WISTMAN'S WOOD.

LEFT: HOUND TOR IS ONE OF DARTMOOR'S BEST VANTAGE POINTS.

ABOVE: AN ANCIENT CLAPPER BRIDGE.

HIGH MOORLAND VISITOR CENTRE

THE OLD DUCHY HOTEL PRINCETOWN YELVERTON PL20 6QF

TEL: 01822 890414

Dunster

Somerset

2 miles (3km) southeast of Minehead

Outstanding in an area known for the beauty of its villages, Dunster has a broad High Street, lined with cottages and former merchants' houses, which leads from the unusual 17th-century octagonal Yarn Market towards

RIGHT: DUNSTER IS THE PERFECT PLACE TO FIND SHOPS PACKED WITH UNUSUAL TREASURES.

the entrance of Dunster Castle. The castle has been the home of the Luttrell family for 600 years. Between 1868 and 1872 the architect Anthony Salvin attuned the castle for comfortable living, but retained the 17th-century plasterwork and oak staircase.

St George's Church, once a Benedictine priory and a parish church, is the largest in Exmoor and dates from the 15th century.

Subtropical plants flourish in the 28-acre (11.2ha) park and the terraced gardens are noted for their exotica, which include a giant lemon tree, yuccas, mimosa and a variety of palms.

LEFT: THE PICTURESQUE APPEARANCE OF DUNSTER CASTLE, IS DUE TO 19TH-CENTURY REMODELLING.

TOURIST INFORMATION CENTRE

17 FRIDAY STREET
MINEHEAD
TA24 5UB

TEL: 01643 702624

Cheddar Gorge

Somerset

8 miles (13km) northwest of Wells

A dramatic natural spectacle, enjoyed either by a drive along the road, a walk along the top or a tour of the adjoining limestone caves, Cheddar Gorge cuts dramatically through the Mendip Hills for nearly 2 miles (3km). It is thought to have been formed by meltwater during the various Ice Ages over the past two million years. The B3135 road winds along the foot of the gorge, with numerous stopping places from where to admire the scene. Cave systems riddle the gorge. The Cheddar Caves feature two show caves – Gough's Cave and Cox's Cave – with richly coloured rock formations, stalagmites and stalactites.

The tourism industry started in the 17th century and has left the village of Cheddar with an abundance of souvenir and cream-tea shops. In centuries past the caves formed the ideal conditions for maturing cheese and, while most Cheddar cheese is now manufactured elsewhere (not just in Britain), you can still see it being made at the Cheddar Cheese Dairy and Craft Village, near the entrance to the gorge.

About 6 miles (9.5km) south are Wookey Hole Caves, where you take a 40-minute guided tour. The first cave dive was made in the Witch's Parlour in 1935, and 25 caverns have since been discovered. Features of the Wookey Hole Caves are the River Axe ravine and the Victorian papermill (handmade paper), a mirror maze and old-fashioned pier amusements.

CHEDDAR CAVES
AND GORGE

CHEDDAR
BS27 3QF

TEL: 01934 742343

RIGHT: TOWERING
LIMESTONE CLIFFS
ENCLOSE THE DEEP AND
WINDING RAVINE OF
CHEDDAR GORGE.

Lyme Regis
Dorset
9 miles (14km) west of Bridport

TOURIST INFORMATION
  CENTRE

GUILDHALL COTTAGE
CHURCH STREET
LYME REGIS
DT7 3BS

TEL: 01297 442138

On a coastline renowned for its Jurassic fossils – snail-like ammonites can even be spotted embedded in garden walls – is this old port and sedate Regency seaside resort. It has a tangle of narrow streets with galleries, cafés, craft and antiques shops, set above a gently shelving beach. It was the favourite place of Jane Austen (1775–1817), who set part of her novel *Persuasion* here. The snaking breakwater known as The Cobb was where a cloaked Meryl Streep stood in the British movie of *The French Lieutenant's Woman* (1981), based on local historian John Fowles' novel of 1969.

LEFT: A VARIETY OF CRAFT BOB ON THE TRANQUIL WATERS OF LYME REGIS HARBOUR.

BELOW: THE PRETTY TOWN HAS A DRAMATIC BACKDROP OF FOSSIL-RICH CLIFFS.

Abbotsbury

Dorset

8 miles (13km) northwest of Weymouth

TOURIST INFORMATION CENTRE

KING'S STATUE
THE ESPLANADE
WEYMOUTH DT4 7AN

TEL: 01305 785747

Thatched ironstone cottages line the streets of this village. Beyond, a huge 15th-century tithe barn and the hilltop St Catherine's Chapel of c1400 are tangible reminders of the Benedictine abbey, founded in 1026, that gave the village its name. Built in the 15th century to store one-tenth of all local produce that was harvested, the abbey barn is now a children's themed play area.

Abbotsbury Swannery, set up by monks in the 14th century, gives unrivalled opportunities to see mute swans close up. Hatching is from mid-May to the end of June, and cygnets gain their wings during September and October; the swans build their nests in March and April.

West of the village, the Sub Tropical Gardens are awash with colour, as late spring brings an abundance of camellias, rhododendrons and heavily perfumed magnolias.

LEFT: A WARDEN WITH ONE OF HIS CHARGES AT THE ABBOTSBURY SWANNERY, SET UP IN THE 14TH CENTURY.

FAR LEFT: THE HUGE 15TH-CENTURY TITHE BARN NOW HOUSES A RURAL DISPLAY.

FAR LEFT: BRIGHTLY
COLOURED BEACH
ACCESSORIES.
LEFT: FISHING FOR
TIDDLERS.
RIGHT: A PUNCH AND
JUDY SHOW

Seaside Holidays

The holiday by the sea is a modern invention. Down into the 18th century, the sea was generally distrusted as a dangerous and disagreeable element. A change of attitude stemmed from a concern with health. The beneficial effects of sea water and fresh sea air were promoted by seaside doctors.

The immediate ancestor of today's seaside resort was the spa. Towns like Bath, Harrogate and Tunbridge Wells offered a combination of healthful mineral waters and smart socialising. Scarborough was a spa which happened to be by the sea, and by 1735 visitors were nervously entering the briny. The new fad spread to Brighton, which by personal appointment to the future King George IV blossomed as the smartest of resorts. His father, George III, went to Weymouth for his health in 1789 and the grateful town prospered as a resort.

From the 1840s on, as the railways spread their tentacles to almost every corner of the country, visitors could reach even remote spots. Places with sandy beaches had a natural advantage, from Newquay to Ayr. So did places with a high sunshine count, such as Torquay and the Isle of Wight resorts.

The railways made it possible for ordinary working people to get away to the seaside for a day and, as holidays steadily lengthened, for a week or more. Resorts like Blackpool, Clacton and Skegness swelled out into cheerful, noisy, unabashedly vulgar magnets for the masses, with piers, funfairs, seaside rock and jellied eels, saucy postcards and variety shows. Perhaps the traditional seaside resort will become a thing of the past, but it was fun while it lasted.

LEFT: BEACH HUTS IN THE BEST LOCATONS CAN COST AS MUCH AS A REAL HOUSE

FAR LEFT: ENJOYING A TRADITIONAL FUNFAIR ON THE SANDS.
LEFT: SEARCHING FOR THE BEST SURFING

ABOVE: SAND-SURFING ALLOWS YOU TO GET UP SPEED.

BELOW: A SLOWER PACE ON THE DONKEY-RIDE.

Chesil Beach
Dorset

TOURIST INFORMATION CENTRE

KING'S STATUE
THE ESPLANADE WEYMOUTH
DT4 7AN

TEL: 01305 785747

This huge wall of shingle – 18 miles (30km) long, up to 49ft (15m) high and more than 525ft (160m) wide – is one of the south coast's major natural features, and is famous for its colony of terns. Stormy seas and strong currents pile pebbles on the bank, from pea-sized stones at the western end of the bank increasing in size to large cobbles in the east. The beach is separated from the mainland by a channel and tidal lagoon called The Fleet, and joins the mainland at Abbotsbury (see page 17). Swimming at any time is extremely unsafe.

ABOVE AND LEFT: THE LONG BAR OF CHESIL BEACH IS CHARACTERIZED BY ITS PEBBLES.

Wells
Somerset
17 miles (24km) south of Bristol

TOURIST INFORMATION
CENTRE

TOWN HALL
MARKET PLACE
WELLS BA5 2RB

TEL: 01749 672552

LEFT: A VIEW OF THE CATHEDRAL'S RICHLY CARVED WEST FRONT.

BELOW: THE CATHEDRAL STANDS BESIDE ST ANDREW'S WELL.

England's smallest city, Wells, lies beneath the southern slopes of the Mendip Hills. Here, the unspoiled perfection of an entire range of ecclesiastical buildings is set around a green at the top of the main street.

The glories of Wells Cathedral begin with its extraordinarily ornate west front (mid-13th century) decorated with more than 400 separate statues, originally in vivid colours and gold. The severe Early English nave is dominated by two unique curving scissor arches, boldly crossing it and interrupting the view. These were added in the 14th century to strengthen the base of the sinking central tower. A well-worn flight of stone steps leads off the north transept to the octagonal chapter house.

Next to the cathedral, the 13th-century Bishop's Palace is still the private residence of the Bishop of Bath and Wells and has imposing state rooms. Surrounded by a moat with swans and set in landscaped gardens (which include the ruins of the Great Hall), it is accessed by the drawbridge and gatehouse.

Other sights worth visiting include the Wells Museum, housed in a Tudor building, which records the area's history, and the late 14th-century Vicar's Close, which is considered to be the oldest complete medieval street in Europe.

Bath
Bath & NE Somerset
11 miles (18km) southeast of Bristol

BATH TOURISM PLUS

ABBEY CHAMBERS
ABBEY CHURCH YARD
BATH BA1 1LY

TEL: 0906 711 2000

It is difficult to imagine a more beautiful city than Bath – great architecture, plenty to see and compact enough to explore on foot – and its World Heritage Site status has ensured its preservation. The city is built from eye-pleasing, honey-coloured limestone, and has a striking setting amid seven hills, where the Cotswolds meet the Mendip Hills, and on the banks of the River Avon and the Kennet and Avon Canal.

Bath was founded by the Romans in AD44 as the settlement of Aquae Sulis. The town prospered through the wool trade in medieval times, but its modern importance dates from the 18th century, after its Roman hot springs were rediscovered in 1755.

With over 20 museums and historic sites, a huge choice of accommodation and many specialist shops, including an antiques market in Bartlett Street, there is something for everyone.

THE PUMP ROOM AND ROMAN BATHS

The high-ceilinged, chandelier-lit Georgian Pump Room (1796) is a great Bath institution, where a chamber trio provides accompaniment to afternoon tea (or you can sample the hot spa water, which may be an acquired taste), within sight of the King's Bath. This room was originally built for a serious purpose – a group of doctors, led by William Oliver (inventor of the Bath Oliver biscuit), felt that invalids should be able to come together to drink Bath's mineral waters. But Richard 'Beau' Nash, the city's Master of Ceremonies, had greater ambitions. Realizing that a Pump Room could be useful as a social centre, he hired a band of musicians to play and soon fashionable visitors were flocking in each morning with their friends.

From the genteel elegance of the Georgian Pump Room you suddenly walk into Roman times in the finest bath-house site in Britain. A self-guiding tour leads past displays of finds from the site down to the actual waters. The highlights of the visit are the pool itself and the Roman Bath (known as the Great Bath) next to it. The spring, still bubbling up in its pool at a constant 46.5°C (116°F), was sacred to the goddess, Sulis, who was thought to possess curative powers.

BATH ABBEY

Not in fact an abbey but a church, this building (begun in 1499) represents one of the crowning examples of the Perpendicular style. Legend has it that the shape of the church was dictated by angels in a dream to its founder, Bishop Oliver King. This story is immortalized on the west front, which shows carved angels ascending and descending on ladders, and the founder's signature – a carving of olive trees surmounted by crowns.

NO. 1 ROYAL CRESCENT

Offering a chance to see inside one of the town houses in Bath's most celebrated architectural set piece, this house was designed (1767–74) by John Wood the Younger. It has been restored to its appearance of 200 years ago, with pictures, china and furniture of the period and a kitchen complete with dog-powered spit to roast meat in front of the fire.

OTHER HIGHLIGHTS

Bath has a range of fascinating museums and points of interest for the visitor, including the Jane Austen Centre, where an exhibition charts the life and works of the great novelist (1775–1817), and the Building of Bath Museum, which explains how Bath developed into the place it is today.

Stourhead
Wiltshire
3 miles (5km) northwest of Mere

THE NATIONAL TRUST
STOURHEAD ESTATE OFFICE

STOURTON
NEAR MERE
WARMINSTER BA12 6QD

TEL: 01747 841152

BELOW AND RIGHT:
STOURHEAD GARDENS
ARE GLORIOUS TO VISIT
THROUGHOUT THE YEAR.

The estate centres on a Palladian-style mansion which was built between 1721 and 1725 by the Scottish architect Colen Campbell (1679–1726).

The mansion is crammed with treasures that include the Regency library, paintings by Canaletto (the nickname of Antonio Canale) and Sir Joshua Reynolds, and furniture designed by Thomas Chippendale (1718–79).

Henry Hoare II, son of a wealthy banker, inspired by his tour of Europe, laid out pleasure gardens between 1741 and 1780. They are a stunning attraction in their own right and feature the Pantheon and Temple of Apollo, a grotto, and a temple to Flora, all set around a central lake. There are some beautiful walks on the estate, especially to King Alfred's Tower, a triangular folly made of red brick, which affords great views.

Lulworth Cove
Dorset
5 miles (8km) south of Wool

TOURIST INFORMATION CENTRE

KING'S STATUE
THE ESPLANADE
WEYMOUTH DT4 7AN

TEL: 01305 785747

BELOW, LEFT AND RIGHT:
THE LULWORTH COVE
AREA IS A POPULAR
SEASIDE HOLIDAY
RESORT FOR FAMILIES.

A beauty spot and geology lesson in one, Lulworth Cove – an almost land-locked pool – is a natural harbour, formed by the sea eroding a narrow gap through the limestone cliff and then scooping out the softer rocks behind. West of the Cove are Stair Hole, a natural sculpture made of rock strata, and Durdle Door, a natural limestone arch carved out by the sea.

The wide range of habitats resulting from this geological diversity supports a variety of birdlife: kittiwakes, shags, cormorants and fulmars on the cliffs, along with buzzards, kestrels and occasional peregrines. Lulworth has its own butterfly, the Lulworth Skipper, first discovered in 1832. This small brown-and-black species, seen in the summer, is rare outside Dorset.

At Easter, most weekends in August and at certain other times you are allowed into the Lulworth Army Ranges on the east side of the Cove. This coastal strip extends to Kimmeridge. The army's presence has saved this landscape from modern intrusions; it is a stronghold for plants such as early spider orchid and wild camomile. Walking is tough going, with steep gradients and dizzying drops. You must keep to the paths at all times, as there are unexploded munitions lying around.

Just below the cliffs are the remains of a fossil forest. Trees from the Jurassic period became submerged in a swamp, allowing algae to grow around them, and sediments trapped by the algae hardened into the round limestone 'burrs' seen today.

Corfe Castle
Dorset
6 miles (10km) southeast of Wareham

CORFE CASTLE
NEAR WAREHAM
BH20 5EZ
TEL: 01929 481294

BELOW: THE RUINS OF CORFE CASTLE PERCH ABOVE THE DORSET COUNTRYSIDE.

Reduced to a jagged ruin after a long siege during the English Civil War (1642–48) but still dominating the view from miles around, Corfe Castle stands on a steep mound at a breach in the Purbeck Hills.

The castle was built in Norman times and added to by King John. At the time of its demise the castle was the family seat of royalist Sir John Bankes, Attorney General under Charles I.

His wife, Lady Bankes, was a key part of the defence of the castle against a Cromwellian siege, and the Roundheads were so impressed by her bravery that she was permitted to take the keys to the castle with her when she was defeated.

Much of the grey stone used to build the village of Corfe Castle was quarried from the castle itself. The village has some good tearooms, shops and pubs.

Stonehenge
Wiltshire
2 miles (3km) west of Amesbury

STONEHENGE
SP4 7DE

TEL: 01980 624715;
01980 626267
(RECORDING)

BELOW: A GLORIOUS ORANGE AND YELLOW SUN SETS OVER THE MYSTICAL STONE CIRCLE OF STONEHENGE.

Europe's most famous prehistoric wonder, Stonehenge stands at the centre of a ceremonial landscape containing 450 scheduled ancient monuments. A powerful atmosphere of mystery and awe prevails because so little is known about the site. Was it a temple or a huge astronomical calendar? Why did people build it and how was this great engineering feat achieved?

What you see are the remains of a sequence of monuments erected in three phases between about 3050BC and 1600BC. The outer circular bank and ditch are the oldest parts, probably constructed over 5,000 years ago. About 475 years later a double circle of 80 'bluestones', each weighing up to four tons, was erected. These stones were brought over 200 miles (324km) from the Welsh Preseli Hills. In 1650BC the bluestones were taken down and two rings of sarsen stones, from the nearby Marlborough Downs, were erected as an outer ring of standing stones, with lintels across the top, and an inner horseshoe of five pairs of uprights with lintels. Later still, some of the bluestones were lined up between the two rings of sarsens in a horseshoe.

The largest bluestone – the so-called Altar Stone – was set at the very centre, where it still lies. The Altar Stone draws the eye towards the Heelstone, over the peak of which the sun rises on 21 June, the longest day of the year. This occurrence has led many to believe that the site had a connection with sun worship and there are many visitors on this day.

Salisbury

Wiltshire

82 miles (132km) southwest of London

The tall spire (404ft/123m) announces Salisbury Cathedral from far around. Started in 1220 and completed in only 38 years, it is uniformly Early English (the first period of Gothic architecture before it evolved into the Decorated and then Perpendicular styles). In the north aisle of the nave a dial-less clock dates from 1386 and is probably the oldest mechanism in working order in the world. The miniature fan-vaulted roof in the grilled Audley Chantry is adorned with ancient *roundels* (decorative medallions), while the cloisters are the largest of any English cathedral. The library over the East Walk contains one of the four original copies of the Magna Carta – England's first bill of rights, imposed on King John by rebel barons in 1215.

Outstanding in a city that is already well endowed with fine streets is Cathedral Close – England's largest – whose houses date from the 14th to 18th centuries. Among them is the National Trust's Mompesson House, a fine example of Queen Anne-style architecture. Another house contains the Salisbury and South Wiltshire Museum, with galleries presenting the area's rich prehistoric heritage, including Stonehenge.

Alongside the impressive architecture are huge swathes of green parkland, where you can walk, take a picnic, play tennis and hire a rowing boat for a jaunt on the river, or listen to live music outdoors in summer.

TOURIST INFORMATION CENTRE

FISH ROW
SALISBURY SP1 1EJ

TEL: 01722 334956

RIGHT: SALISBURY CATHEDRAL WAS BUILT IN THE EARLY ENGLISH STYLE.

New Forest

Hampshire

Southwest of Southampton and east of Ringwood

VISITOR INFORMATION
CENTRE

NEW STREET
LYMINGTON SO41 9BH

TEL: 01590 689000

Strikingly remote, grazed by free-ranging ponies and cattle, and one of England's largest stretches of open, undeveloped country, the New Forest is excellent for walking, camping and picnicking. Established in 1079 as a hunting forest for Norman royalty, it has remained largely intact. At Lymington, the Visitor Information Centre has an exhibition on the area.

Some of the most popular attractions lie in the southeastern corner, including Beaulieu, Exbury Gardens and Bucklers Hard, a hamlet with a nautical flavour, and the launching point of several ships from the fleet of Admiral Lord Nelson (1758–1805).

Don't miss the Bolderwood and Rhinefield ornamental drives – roads planted with giant fir, redwood and cypress trees.

ABOVE LEFT: WILDLIFE IN THE FOREST INCLUDES SIKA DEER.

LEFT: NEW FOREST PONIES ROAM FREELY THROUGHOUT THE AREA.

RIGHT: AUTUMN SUNLIGHT DAPPLING THE ANCIENT BEECH TREES OF THE NEW FOREST CREATES AN ALMOST MAGICAL EFFECT.

Winchester

Hampshire

12 miles (19km) north of Southampton

Engand's ancient capital and seat of the Anglo-Saxon kings, Winchester has a compact historic centre that you can easily explore on foot.

The city came to prominence under Alfred the Great, who made it the capital of his Wessex kingdom in the ninth century. The highlight of the city is its medieval cathedral, dating from 1079 to 1404, in Norman to Perpendicular styles.

Close by are the free City Museum and Winchester College, founded in 1382 by William of Wykeham, and Britain's oldest and one of its most prestigious schools. Near the Westgate, the Great Hall (1235) is all that survives of the city's 13th-century Norman castle. Here, you can see King Arthur's Round Table – a resplendent medieval fake.

A mile to the south of the city, the Hospital of St Cross is a 12th-century almshouse, still home to 25 brethren, reached by a tranquil walk across the water meadows.

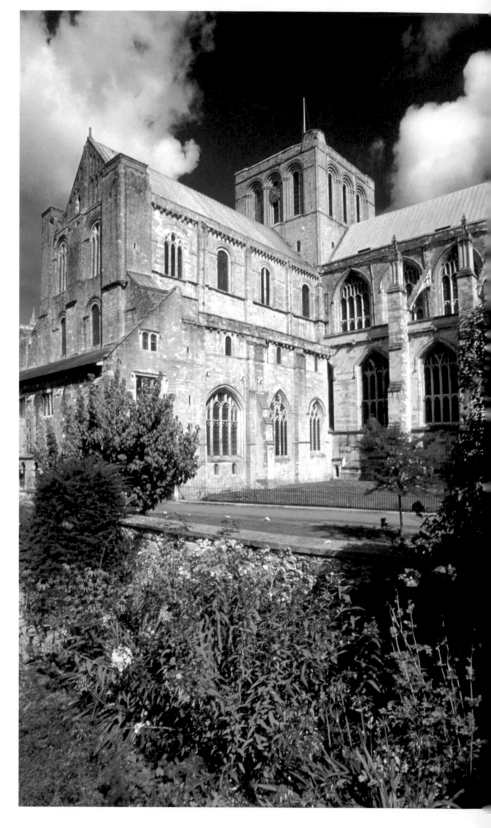

RIGHT: THE CATHEDRAL IS FAMOUS FOR ITS SQUAT CENTRAL TOWER.

LEFT: THE GREAT HALL HOUSES KING ARTHUR'S (FAKE) ROUND TABLE.

TOURIST INFORMATION CENTRE

GUILDHALL
BROADWAY
WINCHESTER SO23 9LJ

TEL: 01962 848427
(RECORDING);
01962 840500

Portsmouth

City of Portsmouth

65 miles (105km) southwest of London

Portsmouth is the home of Britain's naval heritage. It has been a naval base since the 12th century and the centre of one of the most powerful sea-borne fighting forces in history. The city is the home port of the Royal Navy and consequently was heavily bombed during World War II. Historic interest is mostly concentrated around the waterfront.

Not far from Portsmouth Harbour station is the Historic Dockyard with its celebrated warships. Naval officers guide you round Nelson's flagship HMS *Victory* to recall the appalling conditions on board and see the spot where Nelson died in battle in 1805. Close by is the world's first iron-clad battleship, HMS *Warrior*, launched in 1860. Rescued in 1982 after sinking in 1545, Henry VIII's warship *Mary Rose* is constantly sprayed to prevent its timbers from disintegrating; the rich array of finds from the wreck is on display. Also in the dockyard, the Royal Naval Museum charts the history of British maritime defence.

Gunwharf Quays is a mix of designer shopping, eating and drinking places and entertainments, and the venue for international maritime events. At the end of the High Street lies Old Portsmouth, an area of cobbled streets lined with Tudor and Georgian houses. Press gangs once roamed these streets seeking new, but often reluctant, naval recruits.

Portsmouth's first harbour, the Camber, is still a working dock. The Round Tower and Square Tower have guarded the harbour's entrance for 500 years – they are good vantage points.

At Southsea, backed by wide lawns, municipal gardens and Victorian villas, there is a shingle beach. Southsea Castle, on Clarence Esplanade, was built in 1595 to protect Portsmouth against French invasion. Next door, the D-Day Museum and Overlord Embroidery records the largest invasion force ever gathered: for D-Day (6 June 1944). Its focal embroidery measures 83m (272ft) and depicts D-Day scenes.

PORTSMOUTH VISITOR INFORMATION CENTRE

CLARENCE ESPLANADE
SOUTHSEA
PO5 3PB

TEL: 023 9282 6722

ABOVE, RIGHT: OLD PORTSMOUTH CLUSTERS AROUND THE HARBOUR.

RIGHT: HMS *VICTORY* CAN BE FOUND IN THE HISTORIC DOCKYARD.

Isle of Wight
Isle of Wight

ISLE OF WIGHT TOURISM

WESTRIDGE CENTRE
BRADING ROAD
RYDE PO33 1QS

TEL: 01983 813800

RIGHT: OSBORNE HOUSE, QUEEN VICTORIA'S ITALIANATE SEASIDE RETREAT AND FAVOURITE RESIDENCE.

A spectacular coastline, a wide range of family attractions and a mild climate make the Isle of Wight a popular holiday destination. You can leave your car on the mainland as the island has excellent public transport.

THE WEST

Scenery varies from the lonely marshes of the north coast to the southern landslipped cliffs around St Catherine's Point. The best viewpoint of all is Tennyson Down, named after the 19th-century poet who lived near by; a path leads along the ridge to the cliff end above the chalk pinnacles known as The Needles. At Alum Bay a chairlift descends to the beach for close-up views of multi-coloured sand cliffs. On the north coast, Yarmouth is a characterful port with whitewashed cottages and a castle.

THE EAST

This area includes a string of quiet resorts – Ryde, Sandown, Shanklin and Ventnor, with golden sands, calm waters and esplanades. In Ventnor's balmy climate, subtropical species flourish in the Ventnor Botanic Garden. Southeast of the yachting resort of Cowes (which hosts a famous regatta each August) is Osborne House, Queen Victoria's Italianate seaside retreat, which she had built between 1845 and 1851. Outside the island's capital, Newport, Carisbrooke Castle is an impressive Norman ruin, where you can still see the treadwheel that unfortunate prisoners were forced to walk to draw water from the well; later, donkey power was used instead.

Godshill and Shorwell are two of the island's prettiest thatched villages.

ABOVE: THE 15TH-CENTURY TOWER OF ST LAWRENCE'S CHURCH STANDS OVER THE VILLAGE OF GODSHILL.

RIGHT: YACHTING IS PART OF THE CULTURE ON THE ISLAND, WHICH HOSTS THE COWES REGATTA EACH YEAR.

FAR RIGHT: STRIPED DECKCHAIRS ON THE BEACH – A SUMMER SCENE REPEATED ALL OVER BRITAIN'S COAST.

Chichester
West Sussex
9 miles (14km) east of Havant

TOURIST INFORMATION CENTRE

29A SOUTH STREET
CHICHESTER
PO19 1AH

TEL: 01243 775888

BELOW, LEFT:
THE FESTIVAL THEATRE.
BELOW, RIGHT:
THE CATHEDRAL WAS
REBUILT IN 1861–66.

This small, pleasant city still has its original Roman street plan, with two main routes crossing west to east and north to south, enclosed by remains of the city wall (itself partly rebuilt in medieval times). A 16th-century market cross marks the centre point. Close by, the cathedral, smaller than most, is early Norman in style, with Early English additions. The cathedral has an unusual detached belfry, a tapestry by English artist John Piper (1903–92) and stained glass created by the French painter Marc Chagall (1887–1985).

During the 18th century, Chichester was enhanced by such buildings as Pallant House, now a museum with an outstanding collection of British modern art.

West of the city is Fishbourne Roman Palace, the largest known Roman residence in Britain, built about AD75. Much of the villa has been excavated and rooms have been built over the museum to protect the delicate remains from the weather. The palace has the largest collection of in-situ mosaics in Britain and a Roman garden replanted to the original first-century plan.

RHS Garden Wisley

Surrey

3 miles (5km) east of Woking

ROYAL HORTICULTURAL SOCIETY
GARDEN WISLEY

WOKING GU23 6QB

TEL: 01483 224234

BELOW: THE EXTENSIVE LAWNS, SPECIMEN TREES AND BLOOOMS OF WISLEY PROVIDE A GREEN HAVEN.

The Royal Horticultural Society's 250-acre (100ha) garden at Wisley contains a whole range of different habitats, and has much to delight and interest in different seasons, giving a stunning display all year round. Its Alpine Meadow is carpeted with wild daffodils in spring; Battleston Hill is clothed in colourful rhododendrons in early summer; it has heathers and autumnal tints, trial grounds and model gardens. The exotic greenhouse collections (including orchids and fuchsias) offer a haven of warmth on chilly winter days. The garden is also a source of practical advice and the exemplar of best horticultural practice.

The tiny hamlet of Wisley is a charming survival, its centrepiece a tiny church dating from about 1250.

Windsor

Windsor & Maidenhead

2 miles (3km) south of Slough

ROYAL WINDSOR INFORMATION
CENTRE

24 HIGH STREET
WINDSOR SL4 1LH

TEL: 01753 743900

BELOW, LEFT:
THE CASTLE PERCHES
ABOVE THE THAMES.

BELOW, RIGHT:
REGIMENTAL BANNERS AT
ST GEORGE'S CHAPEL.

Windsor is easily explored on foot and has plenty of attractions to fill a whole day. The town's historic grandeur is apparent immediately on arrival.

WINDSOR CASTLE

Windsor Castle sits above the town on a chalk cliff overlooking the River Thames. It is the largest inhabited castle in the world and has been one of the principal residences of the sovereigns of England since William the Conqueror (1027–87) built it. Much of the present-day structure, however, dates from the 19th century. There are several buildings to visit within the castle complex, including St George's Chapel, built between 1475 and 1509; it is a masterpiece of Perpendicular Gothic architecture. The baroque State Apartments, restored following the fire of 1992, are hung with works from the Royal Collection, with drawings and paintings by Michelangelo, Canaletto and many others.

WINDSOR TOWN

The Guildhall on the High Street was completed in 1707 by Christopher Wren. Further up is the 19th-century parish church of St John the Baptist. From here you can continue up Park Street to the Long Walk, which skirts Windsor Great Park. This 3-mile (4.8-km) avenue was laid out by Charles I and planted with elms. Within the park is the 35-acre (14-ha) woodland Savill Garden, worth visiting at any time of the year, but particularly beautiful in spring when the azaleas and camellias are in bloom.

Hever Castle
Kent
2 miles (3km) southeast of Edenbridge

BELOW: HENRY VIII WOOED ANNE BOLEYN AT HEVER CASTLE, HER CHILDHOOD HOME.

HEVER CASTLE
NEAR EDENBRIDGE
TN8 7NG
TEL: 01732 865224

Hever Castle – part doubled-moated 13th-century castle and part Tudor manor house – was the childhood home of Henry VIII's second wife, the doomed Anne Boleyn (1501–36). She lived here with her family until she married the king in 1533.

The castle owes much of its present appearance to lavish early 20th-century renovations by American-born British newspaper magnate William Waldorf Astor (1848–1919), who bought the castle and added mock medieval features and an entire neo-Tudor village behind it for servants and guests. In the gatehouse is an alarming array of instruments of discipline, torture and execution. The Astor family adorned the grounds with formal Tudor, rose and Italian gardens, yew topiary in the form of chessmen, a yew maze and a water maze.

Brighton
Brighton & Hove
48 miles (77km) south of London

Brighton is probably Britain's liveliest seaside resort, raucous but bohemian, with top arts and clubbing venues and some fanciful Regency architecture.

Once a humble fishing village, the town developed a reputation for glamour and flamboyance in the late 18th century when the Prince Regent, later George IV (1762–1830), first visited and started a trend for seaside holidays and sea-bathing. The Royal Pavilion, the King's palace (1815–23), is an oriental

extravaganza bristling with Indian-style minarets and onion domes. The carefully restored interior is famed for its sumptuous decor and elaborate chinoiserie. The former royal stable block now houses the Dome concert hall and the free Brighton Museum and Art Gallery, with lively exhibits on Brighton's social history, and collections of art nouveau furniture as well as 20th-century fashion.

Behind the elegant sweep of Regency terraces on the sea front are The Lanes, a warren of narrow streets and alleys with smart antiques, gifts and designer clothing shops, pavement cafés, restaurants and galleries. North Laine, tucked between The Lanes and the station, is crammed with more than 300 totally individual shops, from 1950s kitsch to funky fashions, plus cafés and pubs.

Architecturally, the West Pier (1866) was Britain's finest, but is closed, having been almost totally destroyed by fire and the sea. The popular Brighton Pier pulsates with seaside amusements.

LEFT: THE ORIENTAL-STYLE ROYAL PAVILION IS AN ASTONISHING SIGHT TO ENCOUNTER IN THE CENTRE OF THE TOWN.

BRIGHTON & HOVE VISITOR INFORMATION SERVICE

10 BARTHOLOMEW SQUARE BRIGHTON BN1 1JS TEL: 0906 711 2255

ABOVE: STRIPED DECKCHAIRS ON THE SHINGLE BY THE VICTORIAN BRIGHTON PIER.

South Downs
East Sussex

SEVEN SISTERS COUNTRY PARK
VISITOR CENTRE

EXCEAT BN25 4AD

TEL: 01323 870280

BELOW: A WINDMILL PUNCTUATES THE LANDSCAPE OF THE SOUTH DOWNS WAY.

BOTTOM: THIS FLINT-WALLED STREET IN FULKING IN THE SOUTH DOWNS HAS HARDLY CHANGED IN 400 YEARS.

The high chalk ridge of the South Downs ends at the south coast in spectacular style with a range of dazzling white cliffs at Beachy Head and the Seven Sisters. A useful starting point is the visitor centre at Seven Sisters Country Park. You can walk out to Cuckmere Haven, the village green at East Dean and to Birling Gap, where steps lead to a pebble beach. A path heads along the clifftops, but keep away from the edge, as the cliff can crumble away without warning.

The South Downs Trust has acquired much of this coast and its hinterland over the years, preserving and restoring the traditional old farming patterns.

Exploring Carisbrooke's Medieval Castle

Isle of Wight

Combine an invigorating downland walk with a visit to a magnificent castle and discover more about Charles I, Carisbrooke's famous prisoner.

Carisbrooke's Medieval Castle Set on a sweeping ridge of chalk downland, 46m (150ft) above the village on the site of a Roman fort, the majestic medieval ruins of Carisbrooke Castle are regarded as one of the Isle of Wight's finest treasures. Originally a fortified camp built by the Saxons as defence against the Vikings, and later strengthened by the Normans, who built the impenetrable stone walls, magnificent gatehouse and fine keep, it overlooks the Bowcombe Valley and the approaches to the central downs and the heart of the island. The castle only experienced military action twice, in 1136 and in 1377.

In the late 16th century the outer bastions were built to guard against the threat of Spanish invasion. The most important episode in the castle's long history was the imprisonment there of Charles I in 1647. You can walk the lofty battlements in the footsteps of Charles I, view the bowling green created for his amusement in the outer bailey, and see the window from which he tried to escape.

LEFT: A TUDOR-COSTUMED GUIDE SETS THE SCENE.

RIGHT: ENTERING THROUGH THE VENERABLE GATEWAY.

The Rise and Fall of Charles I There had been an uneasy relationship between Crown and Parliament during the reign of James I, and after the accession to the throne of his son, Charles I, in 1625 things went from bad to worse. Charles's High Church views and demands for war funds provoked a series of crises and disputes, and in 1630 he dispensed with Parliament altogether and embarked on a period of personal rule.

After nearly a decade, Charles's lack of empathy, stubbornness and high-minded approach to statecraft led to the collapse of royal authority and the descent into rebellion and civil war by 1642. Bitter battles between the Royalist and Parliamentarian armies raged across the country for four years, until major strategic errors by Charles led to crushing defeats at Naseby, Langport, Bristol and, finally, at Oxford in

RIGHT: STONE WALLS FORMED THE OUTER DEFENCES OF THE CASTLE.

BELOW: THE LIGHT AND AIRY PRIVATE CHAPEL HOUSES AN ETHEREALLY BEAUTIFUL ALTARPIECE.

May 1646, Charles still considered it his divine right to rule, and he refused to negotiate a political settlement with the Parliamentarians.

Rumours spread of a plot to murder him, and Charles escaped from Hampton Court Palace in 1647 and sought refuge at Carisbrooke Castle. Governor Robert Hammond was torn between his loyalty to the king and his duty to Parliament, but promised to do what he could for Charles. He was treated with respect, had the best rooms in the castle and was allowed freedom to move around the island. On hearing that Charles had signed a secret treaty with the Scots in December 1647, Hammond imprisoned Charles in the castle. During his ten-month incarceration Charles made two unsuccessful attempts to escape before being taken to London for trial and execution in 1648.

Exploring Carisbrooke Castle's Downland Vista

❶ Facing Carisbrooke Priory, turn left along the road and take the footpath, opposite Quarr Business Park, to Carisbrooke Castle – built on a Roman site Carisbrooke once marked the capital of the island. At the castle walls, follow the grassy rampart right around the walls, continuing past the castle entrance. Take the footpath, signed Millers Lane, to the right of the car park entrance and descend to a lane. Turn left, cross a ford, then at a T-junction, turn right to Froglands Farm. Pass the farm, then bear right at gates to follow a bridleway through Bowcombe Valley.

❷ After a sharp right bend, gently descend and cross the stile on your left. Keep straight on, following the grassy path to a track. Turn left and keep right at a fork. At the field boundary on the left, follow the field edge to a gate. Ascend through a copse to a gate, then keep to the left-hand field edge, steadily uphill to a gate. Maintain direction to a further gate. Keep to the wide track beside a coniferous plantation and take the footpath left, signed Gatcombe. Go through a gate and keep ahead, passing a dew pond, to a further gate. On reaching a stile on the left, bear right downhill to a T-junction of paths and turn left, signed Garstons.

❸ Descend off the down. Go through a gate and shortly bear right beside Newbarn Farm. Turn right along the metalled access lane into the hamlet. Keep right on merging with Snowdrop Lane and turn left along the Shepherds Trail, signed Carisbrooke.

❹ Ascend a concrete drive and pass a house. At the top, keep to the main path (Shepherds Trail) across fields via gates. Disregard the path merging from the left and shortly follow the sunken path gently downhill to Whitcombe Road. Keep ahead back to the car park.

Distance: 5.25 miles (9km)

Total ascent: 600ft (183m)

Paths: generally firm but can be muddy in wet weather

Terrain: farmland and open downland

Gradients: undulating; one steep ascent and one long steady climb

Refreshments: Coach House tea room at Carisbrooke Castle

Castle: Open all year daily, except at Christmas and New Year. Tel: 01983 522107

OS Map: OS Outdoor Leisure 29 Isle of Wight

Rye & Winchelsea

East Sussex

9 miles (14km) northeast of Hastings

Rye and Winchelsea are two captivating historic gems, rich in domestic architecture. Just 2 miles (3km) apart, the towns were medieval Cinque Ports, part of a confederation that supplied ships to the navy in return for privileges from the monarch. Since then, the sea has receded, leaving shingle beaches and two small towns seemingly suspended in time.

The larger of the two, Rye, is a huddle of cobbled streets, medieval half-timbered, red-tiled houses and elegant Georgian buildings. The town's antiques shops and galleries are great for browsing. Parts of the 14th-century defences still remain, notably the Landgate Arch and Ypres Tower, a former lookout dating from 1249, now housing the Rye Castle Museum. Facing the church, in West Street, is the early 18th-century Lamb House, home of the American novelist Henry James (1843–1916) from 1898 until his death. It was later occupied by author E. F. Benson.

Winchelsea, the smallest town in England (population 400), began life at sea level until its destruction in a storm in 1287. It was rebuilt to a grid pattern (the first example of town planning in medieval England) on the clifftop, fortified with walls and gateways against French invaders. Most buildings have 17th- and 18th-century façades, although many are much older. Only the choir and chapels remain of St Thomas's Church; its 20th-century stained-glass windows tell the town's story. The medieval Court Hall, restored in the 16th century, houses the local museum.

LEFT: BOATS CLUSTER IN THE HARBOUR.

ABOVE: MERMAID STREET MAKES REGULAR APPEARANCES AS A FILM AND TV SET.

RYE HERITAGE CENTRE
STRAND QUAY
RYE TN31 7AY

TEL: 01797 226696

Canterbury

Kent

54 miles (87km) southeast of London

Despite the damage of a World War II bombing raid in 1942, much remains of the medieval city that was a centre of pilgrimage to the shrine of the English saint, Thomas Becket. Archbishop Becket was murdered in Canterbury Cathedral on the orders of King Henry II in 1170. The pilgrims' journey was immortalized by poet Geoffrey Chaucer (c1342–1400) in *The Canterbury Tales*, begun in the 1380s.

Seat of the Archbishop of Canterbury (head of the Church of England), the cathedral, approached via the ornate 16th-century Christ Church Gate, dates from about 1070. Its main glory is the 12th-century stained glass showing pilgrim scenes. In the northwest transept, a stone marks the spot where Becket died.

Several charitable hospitals founded in medieval times to accommodate pilgrims include Eastbridge Hospital and the Poor Priests' Hospital, which now houses the Museum of Canterbury, a modern exploration of 2,000 years of the city's history.

CANTERBURY INFORMATION CENTRE

12–13 BUTTERMARKET
SUN STREET
CANTERBURY CT1
2HX

TEL: 01227 378100

ABOVE: THE FAMOUS CATHEDRAL CAN BE APPROACHED THROUGH A GATEHOUSE (LEFT) IN THE CENTRAL SQUARE.

Medieval city walls enclose three sides of Canterbury and its narrow, crooked alleys, lined with leaning timbered buildings. One original 14th-century gate, West Gate, survives. The underground Roman Museum, in Longmarket, has the remains of a Roman house and recreated interiors. Outside the city are the ruins of St Augustine's Abbey, founded in AD597.

Buckingham Palace
London

Buckingham Palace is a world-famous symbol of monarchy and focus for ceremonial and public occasions, as well as one of Queen Elizabeth II's main official residences.

The palace, so familiar to millions from newsreels and postcards, has had centuries of piecemeal architectural changes. Originally plain Buckingham House, it was built in 1702 for the Duke of Buckingham. King George III snapped it up as a private residence in 1761 and work began on embellishments and additions. When Queen Victoria and Prince Albert moved into the palace in 1837, a whole new wing was added to house their

fast-growing family, closing off the three-sided quadrangle and removing the Marble Arch that provided its grand entrance. The present forecourt, where Changing the Guard takes place, was formed in 1911, as part of the Victoria Memorial scheme.

TICKET SALES AND
  INFORMATION OFFICE
BUCKINGHAM PALACE
LONDON SW1A 1AA
TEL: 0207 766 7300

TOP: THE CEREMONY OF THE CHANGING OF THE GUARD IS ONE OF LONDON'S MAJOR TOURIST ATTRACTIONS.

ABOVE: ONE OF THE MOST FAMOUS FAÇADES IN THE WORLD – THE EAST FRONT OF BUCKINGHAM PALACE.

Hampstead
London

Hampstead Heath is a wonderfully diverse public open space of 790 acres (320ha). Londoners come here to exercise, picnic and swim in the three ponds. East of the ponds is Parliament Hill, a steep incline with extensive views over the city.

At the northern end is Kenwood House, built in 1616 and remodelled by Robert Adam in 1764 for the Earl of Mansfield. Left to the nation in 1927 by the first Earl of Iveagh, it has an outstanding collection of paintings by English and Dutch masters.

The poet John Keats (1795–1821) came to live here in 1818. During his time at what is now known as Keats' House in Keats' Grove (in 1820 he left for Italy for health reasons), he wrote some of his best-loved poems, including 'Ode to a Nightingale'.

Built in 1695, Fenton House, on Windmill Hill, has period furnishings complemented by a collection of ceramics and 17th-century needlework and the Benton Fletcher Collection of 17th- and 18th-century instruments. No. 2 Willow Road, designed in the 1930s by Ernö Goldfinger, and London's only Modernist house open to the public, houses works by British and European 20th-century artists, including Henry Moore.

Sigmund Freud (1856–1939), the founder of psychoanalysis, lived at 20 Maresfield Gardens, Hampstead, from 1938, after escaping from Nazi-occupied Vienna. Freud's House and Museum, devoted to his life and work, displays his famous analysis couch.

HAMPSTEAD HEATH
  INFORMATION CENTRE

PARLIAMENT HILL STAFF YARD
HIGHGATE ROAD
LONDON NW5 1QR

TEL: 0207 482 7073

ABOVE, RIGHT:
HAMPSTEAD HEATH,
HAS LONG PROVIDED
LONDONERS WITH
A PLACE TO RELAX.

St Paul's Cathedral
London

The first St Paul's, built in AD604, was rebuilt 300 years later after a Viking attack and replaced by a Norman cathedral, Old St Paul's, in 1087. After its destruction in the Great Fire of 1666, Sir Christopher Wren (1632–1723) was commissioned to build a new one. Wren's masterpiece, completed in 1710, is a combination of vast, airy spaces and elaborate decoration.

Eight pillars support the huge dome, 364ft (111m) high and weighing in the region of 65,000 tonnes. The accoustics in the Whispering Gallery enable you to hear someone whispering on the far side, after a few seconds' delay. The frescoes on the dome depict scenes from the life of St Paul and were painted by Sir James Thornhill between 1716 and 1719. The Golden Gallery runs around the outer dome, a breathtaking 280ft (85m) from the cathedral floor. A hole in the floor gives a dizzying view down.

The chancel is a riot of 19th-century Byzantine gilding. In the north choir aisle is a marble sculpture, *Mother and Child*, by Henry Moore (1898–1986). The marble effigy of poet John Donne (1572–1631), in the south choir aisle, is one of the few effigies that survived the Great Fire of London in 1666.

The Duke of Wellington (1769–1852), who was a Napoleonic War hero and prime minister 1828–30, lies in a simple Cornish granite casket. Admiral Nelson (1758–1805), who died in action at the Battle of Trafalgar, lies at the centre of the crypt.

LEFT: THE DISTINCTIVE DOME OF ST PAUL'S CATHEDRAL IS THE THIRD LARGEST IN THE WORLD.

ABOVE: TOMBS AND MEMORIALS INSIDE PAY HOMAGE TO MANY NOTABLE AND TALENTED INDIVIDUALS.

ST PAUL'S COURTYARD
LONDON
EC4M 8AD

TEL: 020 7246 8348

Tower of London
London

TOWER OF LONDON LONDON EC3N 4AB

TEL: 0870 756 6060 (RECORDING); 0870 756 7070 (TICKETS)

BELOW, RIGHT: THE YEOMAN WARDERS OR 'BEEFEATERS' HAVE BEEN GUARDING THE TOWER SINCE 1485.

BOTTOM: THE WHITE TOWER IS ONE OF LONDON'S MOST FAMOUS HISTORICAL LANDMARKS.

The Tower of London is a symbol of 1,000 years of Britain's royal history. In past centuries, prisoners accused of treason would enter the Tower of London through Traitors' Gate – some, such as Henry VIII's second wife, Anne Boleyn, taking their final journey. Today the visitors' entrance is through the Middle Tower.

At the heart of the Tower is its oldest medieval building, the White Tower, thought to date from 1078 and built to serve as a fortress and a royal residence. There's an exhibition about small arms from the Royal Armouries collection, and spiral stairs lead to the glorious Chapel of St John the Evangelist. John Flamsteed (1646–1719), Charles II's astronomer, observed the stars from the turrets before moving to new headquarters at Greenwich.

A range of displays in the Jewel House tell the history of the Coronation Regalia (Crown Jewels), which are kept in the treasury. The jewels date mainly from the restoration of the monarchy in 1660, when Charles II came to the throne. Among the priceless stones in the collection is the world's biggest cut diamond, the 530-carat First Star of Africa.

Many famous prisoners, including Anne Boleyn, have been incarcerated and executed here. The Bloody Tower gets its name from the supposed murder of the two princes, Edward and Richard, by their uncle, Richard III. The Queen's House was the scene of Guy Fawkes' interrogation in 1605. High-ranking prisoners were kept in the 13th-century Beauchamp Tower.

ENTRY TO THE TRAITORS GATE

TIDY THAMES I

Shakespeare's Globe
London

BELOW: A STEP BACK
IN TIME TO THE
ELIZABETHAN ERA AT
THE RECONSTRUCTED
GLOBE THEATRE.

21 NEW GLOBE WALK
BANKSIDE
LONDON SE1 9DT

TEL: 020 7902 1400;
020 7401 9919 (BOX
OFFICE)

The original Globe was one of the first purpose-built theatres in the country, built in 1599 by a company that included William Shakespeare. It was destroyed by fire during a production of *Hamlet* in 1613. A project began in 1969 to create an accurate, functioning reconstruction, using materials, tools and techniques closely matching those of Elizabethan times, but it was 1997 before it was finished.

The theatre is built of unseasoned oak and held together with 6,000 oak pegs. It is crowned with the first thatched roof to be built in the city (understandably) since the Great Fire in 1666. In the centre, an elevated stage and an open-air yard are surrounded on three sides by covered tiers of benches that seat 1,500. Productions are held in the afternoon during the summer, much as in Shakespeare's day, subject to fine weather.

Westminster Abbey
London

WESTMINSTER ABBEY
INFORMATION DESK

c/o THE CHAPTER OFFICE
20 DEAN'S YARD
LONDON SW1P 3PA

TEL: 0207 654 4834

The largest surviving medieval church in London, Westminster Abbey has been the setting for all royal coronations since 1066 and its mausoleum commemorates 3,300 of the nation's most famous historical figures. You enter by the north transept, then turn left to take a one-way, clockwise tour of the church and cloisters. North of the sanctuary is the Lady Chapel, where you can view the white-marble effigy of Elizabeth I, who died in 1603. The main part of the chapel, with its fan-vaulted ceiling, is an impressive setting for the royal tombs arranged around the altar and aisles.

The south transept, also known as Poets' Corner, is where great poets, authors, artists and actors have been honoured with memorials. Here are the remains of poet Geoffrey Chaucer (c1345–1400), and William Shakespeare's (1564–1616) monument. The chapter house is an octagonal building of 1253 where Parliament met between 1257 and 1547, before moving to the Palace of Westminster. A few doors down from the abbey itself the abbey museum has macabre wax effigies of Elizabeth I, Charles II and Lord Nelson.

FAR LEFT: TWIN TOWERS MARK THE WEST FRONT OF THE BUILDING.
LEFT: A ROYAL TOMB.

ABOVE: BRIGHT GILDING ON THE CHOIR STALLS.

London Eye
London

The world's largest observation wheel towers 443ft (135m) above the banks of the River Thames, allowing a bird's-eye view over London. The capsules have unobstructed views from large windows and the wheel is in constant, very slow motion. On a clear day you can see all of London's towers and spires beyond the city 25 miles (40km) in each direction. You are recommended to book in advance, especially at peak times.

BRITISH AIRWAYS
LONDON EYE

RIVERSIDE BUILDING
COUNTY HALL
WESTMINSTER BRIDGE
ROAD
LONDON
SE1 7PB

TEL: 0870 500 0600
(BOOKING)

LEFT AND BELOW:
A RIDE ON THE
LONDON EYE GIVES
A UNIQUE PERSPECTIVE
OVER THE CITY.

Hampton Court
London

HAMPTON COURT PALACE

EAST MOLESEY
KT8 9AU

TEL: 0870 753 7777

This magnificent Tudor palace, set in extensive grounds on the banks of the River Thames, was begun in 1514 as a country residence for Cardinal Thomas Wolsey (c1475–1530), Lord Chancellor to Henry VIII. Some fourteen years later, Wolsey was 'encouraged' to present it to the king, and for centuries after it was home to British monarchs. The palace is a mix of styles – extensive Tudor buildings with some late 17th-century baroque additions by Sir Christopher Wren. Costumed guides and audio tours lead the way through endless corridors, grand apartments, lavish bedrooms and vast Tudor kitchens, which remain much as they were when in use. In summer you can arrive by riverboat from Westminster, Richmond or Kingston-upon-Thames. The grounds include a famous maze, planted in 1690, which is fiendishly frustrating.

Pembrokeshire Coast National Park
Southwest Wales

The Pembrokeshire Coast National Park – at 225sq miles (583sq km) one of the smallest of Britain's national parks – is the only one that is largely coastal, and it's not difficult to understand why. Its main glory is its superb 230-mile (370km) coastline, which is followed for 170 miles (274km) of its way by the Pembrokeshire Coast Path, a wonderful rollercoaster of a walk giving much better views of the rugged cliffs, secluded bays and ever-changing seascapes than those you get from the road. The scenery divides between the level cliffs in the south and the more rugged north.

One of many outstanding coastal viewpoints is Wooltack Point near Marloes, which overlooks Skomer and Skokholm islands. Bosherston Lily Ponds lie close to the sandy beach of Broad Haven; the coast path going west passes the rock pillars of Elegug Stacks and the natural arch known as the Green Bridge of Wales. A labyrinth of tidal creeks drains into the harbour of Milford Haven. Overlooking one inlet is Carew Castle, the ruined shell of a medieval fortress turned Elizabethan mansion, close to a tide mill and an 11th-century Celtic cross.

The three ancient, primitive hermitage chapels of St Non, St Justinian (both near St David's) and St Govan (near Bosherston) are each built into remote cliffs.

Near St David's, Whitesands Bay is a long bathing beach. St David's Head, a short walk north, looks across to the Wicklow Mountains in Ireland. Strumble Head, at the tip of a remote section of cliffs, has some of the best views to the south from the Iron Age hillfort site of Garn Fawr. Fishguard is a hilly little harbour town with ferries to Rosslare County Wexford in Ireland.

LEFT: THE PEMBROKESHIRE COAST PATH AFFORDS DRAMATIC VIEWS.

NATIONAL PARK
VISITOR CENTRE

THE GROVE
ST DAVID'S
SA62 6NW

TEL: 01437 720392

The Preseli Hills are dotted with
Bronze Age stone circles and Neolithic
cromlechs (burial chambers). It was from
here that the bluestones of Stonehenge
originated (see page 28). On the hill-fort
site of Castell Henllys is a reconstructed
Iron Age village typical of the area.

LEFT: TENBY HARBOUR IS
OVERLOOKED BY THE
CASTLE REMAINS FROM
THEIR VANTAGE POINT
ON CASTLE HILL.

ABOVE: NEOLITHIC
BURIAL CHAMBERS MAY
BE FOUND AT A RANGE
OF SITES IN THE
NATIONAL PARK AREA.

Laugharne
Carmarthenshire
4 miles (6km) south of Clears

Pronounced 'larn', this quiet town on the Taf Estuary grew up around 12th- to 16th-century Laugharne Castle, now an imposing ruin. The Welsh poet Dylan Thomas (1914–53) settled here in 1949, and the boathouse and writing shed, where he lived and worked in his final, tragic and alcohol-blighted years, make a poignant visit. Creating the right atmosphere is the paper-strewn desk (with discarded papers on the floor) where Thomas wrote his best-known work, *Under Milk Wood* (1954), basing its fictitious town of Llareggub on Laugharne. Both Thomas and his long-suffering wife Caitlin are buried in St Martin's Churchyard.

ABOVE: THIS BOATHOUSE BY THE LAKE PROVIDED A TRANQUIL HOME FOR POET DYLAN THOMAS.

LEFT: LAUGHARNE CASTLE, ONCE THE SCENE OF BATTLES AND SIEGES, IS NOW A ROMANTIC SHELL.

TOURIST INFORMATION CENTRE

113 LAMMAS STREET
CARMARTHEN
SA31 3AQ

TEL: 01267 231557

Caernarfon
Gwynedd
7 miles (11km) southeast of Bangor

TOURIST INFORMATION CENTRE

CASTLE DITCH, CASTLE STREET
CAERNARFON LL55 1SE

TEL: 01286 679600;
01286 672232

BELOW: CAERNARFON CASTLE IS REGARDED AS THE MOST AMBITIOUS FORTRESS BUILT BY EDWARD I.

This market town is dwarfed by the magnificent harbourside Caernarfon Castle, built in 1283 by Edward I (1239–1307) to consolidate his conquest of Wales. Edward I's son, the future Edward II (1284–1327), was born there and made Prince of Wales. In 1969 the castle was the setting for Prince Charles's investiture as Prince of Wales. Substantial lengths of the medieval town wall snake through the town.

On a hill above the town lie the foundations of the Roman settlement fort of Segontium (founded AD77), with a museum displaying finds from this far-flung frontier of the Roman Empire. On Caernarfon Airparc, where the RAF Mountain Rescue Service was formed in 1943, is Caernarfon Airworld Museum, an indoor interactive museum with historic and modern aircraft, trial flights and pleasure flights.

Harlech

Gwynedd

16 miles (25.5km) south of Porthmadog

The walls and six drum towers of this 13th-century castle stand virtually at their original height. Built as one of Edward I's iron ring of fortresses designed to subdue the Welsh, it is defended by a massive gatehouse and commands views of the sea, the Snowdonia mountains and the Lleyn Peninsula. Although the sea has now receded, when the castle was built it had a sheer drop to the water on one side.

The building of the great castle was completed within seven years – a remarkable short time for such a feat of engineering – between 1283 and 1290. Harlech is concentric, with outer walls giving further protection to the inner walls, which contained the main living quarters. The inner walls also contain the great gatehouse, with its comfortable residential appartments. The gatehouse is perhaps the castle's finest feature. Two sides were protected by deep dry moats hacked out of the rock on which the castle stands, while cliffs plunging down to the sea made assault on the back of the castle virtually impossible.

The last great uprising of the Welsh against the occupying English forces occurred under the leadership of the hero Owen Glyndwr. In the spring of 1404, Glyndwr gathered his forces against the mighty fortress of Harlech,

LEFT AND ABOVE:
HARLECH CASTLE,
GUARDED BY ITS
MASSIVE GATEHOUSE,
OCCUPIES THE IDEAL
DEFENSIVE POSITION.

HARLECH CASTLE

CASTLE SQUARE
HARLECH
LL46 2YH

TEL: 01766 780552

but the castle was too strong to be taken in a battle and so Glyndwr began a long siege.

For many months the castle garrison held out, in spite of Glyndwr's efficient blockade of all the castle's supply routes. Food began to run low, and then disease broke out, doubtless aggravated by the shortage of clean water. After some of the soldiers had unsuccessfully tried to escape, Glyndwr stood at the castle gate and demanded surrender.

Harlech was Glyndwr's home and headquarters for the next four years, and it is said that he crowned himself Prince of Wales in Harlech. Finally, in 1409, Henry IV sent a powerful force to recapture the castle and stamp out the rebellion. After a short siege, the castle fell. Glyndwr's wife and children were taken prisoner and, although Glyndwr himself escaped, the fall of Harlech marked the beginning of the end for him. Within four years he had disappeared.

Conwy
Conwy
3 miles (5km) south of Llandudno

BELOW: THE FORMIDABLE
BULK OF CONWY
CASTLE, VIEWED FROM
THE ESTUARY THAT IT
WAS BUILT TO GUARD.

CONWY CASTLE
   VISITOR CENTRE

CONWY
LL32 8LD

TEL: 01492 592248

The best-preserved medieval town in Wales memorably evokes the era of English rule. Conwy was built by Edward I after his conquest of the area in 1283; his military architect, James of St George, created a walled and fortified town modelled on those in Switzerland and France. By the 18th century Conwy had settled into its role as a trading post and river-ferry port on the route to Holyhead and Ireland.

The town's most striking feature is the virtually intact 4,200ft (1,280m) wall that extends from the castle and contours above the streets. Three double-towered gateways and 21 towers punctuate the wall; a walk along it gives wonderful views over the town rooftops, the surrounding countryside and the river.

Also built by Edward I, the formidable castle has eight massive round towers guarding the estuary. Inside, only one stone arch remains of the eight that were constructed in the 1340s to support the roof of the great hall.

One of Conwy's great treasures is Plas Mawr, the Elizabethan town house completed in 1585. Designed to spread up rather than outwards, the house was partly influenced by European architecture. In 1993 the Welsh heritage body Cadw embarked on a meticulous restoration project that resulted in a re-creation of Gwynne's great hall, kitchen, bedrooms and banqueting room, many decorated in elaborate and colourful plasterwork.

On the corner of Castle Street, Aberconwy House, with its external stone steps and overhanging upper storey, represents the sole surviving merchants' building of medieval Conwy. It has period furniture and a video traces its varied history.

On the quayside is the Smallest House, an incredibly narrow one-up, one-down dwelling.

Llandudno
Conwy
5 miles (8km) northwest of Colwyn Bay

TOURIST INFORMATION
CENTRE

1–2 CHAPEL STREET
LLANDUDNO LL30 2SY

TEL: 01492 876413

BELOW: LLANDUDNO, WITH ITS LONG PIER, IS A FAVOURITE PLACE FOR FAMILY SUMMER HOLIDAYS BY THE SEA.

As an example of Victorian seaside architecture, Llandudno has weathered admirably. Its seafront is an elegant curve of hotels and guesthouses overlooking a pebble beach and traditional iron-railed pier. Venture by cable-car or steep tramway to Great Ormes Head for fine views over Conwy Bay and the Snowdonia mountains.

The Great Orme Mines were dug for copper by Bronze Age settlers around 4,000 years ago and claim to be the oldest metal mines in the world open to the public.

Snowdonia
North Wales

RIGHT AND BELOW: THE SNOWDON MOUNTAIN TRAIN HAULS ITS WAY FROM LLANBERIS TO THE MOUNTAIN SUMMIT.

Covering a large chunk of northwest Wales, Snowdonia takes its name from Snowdon (3,560ft/1,085m), the highest point of the Snowdonia National Park and the highest mountain in England and Wales. This remarkably beautiful area of wild peaks and lakes is the second largest national park in Britain after the Lake District and draws great numbers of walkers and climbers, particularly to the area around Snowdon. There are routes of varying difficulties, from gentle strolls in the valleys to much more difficult and more demanding routes on the tops.

Glyder Fawr, Carnedd Dafydd and Moel Siabod are among other shapely peaks, while there are easier walks in the forests around the village of Betws-y-Coed and along the Aberglaslyn Pass near the village of Beddgelert.

Built of sturdy stone around a spacious square, Dolgellau, near the summit of Cadair Idris (2,915ft/889m), is the only town inside the national park. Others lying close to the boundary include the historic castle towns of Caernarfon (see page 57) and Conwy (see page 60) and the Victorian seaside resort of Llandudno (see page 61). Blaenau Ffestiniog has an industrial setting amid mountains of slate scraps, and you can visit slate caverns. The terraced shelves of the Dinorwic Slate Quarry are now the site of the Welsh Slate Museum and one of the most advanced underground hydroelectric schemes in the world.

Restored steam railways run along the lake shores and curve through majestic mountain scenery. The best-known is the Snowdon Mountain Railway from Llanberis to the summit.

SNOWDONIA NATIONAL
PARK AUTHORITY

PENRHYNDEUDRAETH
LL48 6LF

TEL: 01766 770274

RIGHT: LLANBERIS PASS
PROVIDES A CONVENIENT
ROUTE THROUGH THE
MOUNTAINS OF
THE NATIONAL PARK.

Llangollen
Denbighshire
11 miles (18km) east of Corwen

LLANGOLLEN TOURIST
INFORMATION CENTRE
Y CAPEL
LLANGOLLEN LL20 8NU
TEL: 01978 860828

BELOW, LEFT:
LLANGOLLEN'S BRIDGE
OVER THE RIVER DEE
IS ONE OF THE
'WONDERS OF WALES'.

BELOW, RIGHT: THIS
PEACEFUL STRETCH OF
CANAL AT LLANGOLLEN
WAS ONCE PART OF ITS
TRADING ROUTES.

The romantic, green Vale of Llangollen, nestling beneath limestone crags, has attracted tourists since the late 18th century. The market town of Llangollen has been host since 1947 of the International Eisteddfod held each July, when performers from all over the world compete in dance, song and instrumental music. The venue is the impressive Royal International Pavilion. Indoor attractions here include The Victorian School of the 3 Rs and Heritage Centre, depicting the daily life of a 19th-century child, and the Motor Museum and Canal Exhibition, with cars and cycles dating from 1912 and a display about canal-building.

Above the town is Plas Newydd, the home of the Ladies of Llangollen – Lady Eleanor Butler and Miss Sarah Ponsonby – who fled their families in Ireland in order to live together, and who welcomed a stream of celebrated visitors to their cottage between 1780 and 1829. The house is furnished as it was in their day; an exhibition in one room tells the ladies' remarkable story.

The canal wharf is the starting point for horse-drawn barge trips through the vale, including a dizzy stretch across Thomas Telford's monumental Pontcysyllte Aqueduct, 126ft (38m) above the River Dee, and reaching the river at the sweeping weir of Horseshoe Falls. Steam trains on the Llangollen Railway lead through 8 miles (13km) of scenery, stopping at Berwyn, above the river gorge and a 15-minute walk from Horseshoe Falls.

Wide views of the vale beyond Llangollen are had from the ruins of 13th-century Castell Dinas Brân (Crow City Castle). Some 2 miles (3.5km) north of Llangollen are the remains of 13th-century Valle Crucis Abbey. The valley was named after Eliseg's Pillar, a 9th-century Christian memorial near the abbey.

Brecon Beacons
Central South Wales

While lacking the drama of the very highest peaks of Snowdonia National Park (see page 62), these highlands of South Wales have their share of exhilarating walks and views, particularly on the precipitous sandstone ridge that rises to Pen y Fan (2,907ft/886m).

The eastern flanks comprise the Black Mountains, a series of ridges and valleys. Here a road edges past the ruins of 13th-century Llanthony Abbey and over the Gospel Pass to drop steeply to the second-hand bookshop mecca and charming market town of Hay on Wye. The Georgian town of Brecon and its surroundings mark the central ground of the national park and make a good base for visits. To the west is Black Mountain, a bleak moorland expanse dominated by the craggy ridge of Carmarthen Fan. In the south the Waterfall Country is a tremendous series of waterfalls along the gorges of the Hepste, Mellte and Nedd. Head out to Sgwd yr Eira, which is a magnificent waterfall in the Waterfall Country, where you can squeeze your way along a ledge behind the curtain of the fall.

LEFT AND ABOVE: THE LANDSCAPE OF THE BRECON BEACONS HAS SOME DRAMATIC SEASONAL DIFFERENCES.

NATIONAL PARK INFORMATION CENTRE

CATTLE MARKET CAR PARK
BRECON LD3 9DA

TEL: 01874 622485

Cardiff

Cardiff

130 miles (209km) west of London

From its beginnings as the site of a Roman fort on the River Taf (Taff), Cardiff grew up as a village protected by a Norman castle and later became a modest harbour town.

By the early 20th century it was the biggest coal-exporting dock in the world. The city centre has handsome Victorian and Edwardian shopfronts and arcades, a 19th-century covered market and gleaming civic buildings. The redevelopment of the docks area began in the 1980s, and its connection with the centre was gradually re-established. It's now the home of the Welsh National Assembly.

The focus of the city is Cardiff Castle, which is a Norman fortress dating from Roman times. In the 19th century it was transformed into a flamboyant, neo-Gothic extravaganza by the third Marquess of Bute and his medievalist designer William Burges (1827–81).

Northeast of the castle, the white Portland-stone buildings of the Civic Centre, built in the 19th and 20th centuries, are laid out on broad avenues. In front are the elaborate City Hall and the National Museum and Gallery, with an Evolution of Wales exhibition and the largest collection of Impressionist and post-Impressionist paintings outside France.

Cardiff's docks have become vibrant Cardiff Bay, which is fringed with restaurants, bars and shops. Among the attractions are Butetown History and Arts Centre, tracing the area's history; and the Pierhead Building, with a display about the National Assembly for Wales.

LEFT: THE PIERHEAD BUILDING LIES IN CARDIFF'S RESTORED MARITIME AREA, KNOWN AS CARDIFF BAY.

ABOVE: THE NORMAN KEEP AND 13TH-CENTURY TOWER OF CARDIFF CASTLE DOMINATE THE TOWN.

CARDIFF VISITOR CENTRE

THE OLD LIBRARY
THE HAYES
CARDIFF CF10 1AH

TEL: 029 2022 7281

Castell Coch
Cardiff
5 miles (8km) northwest of Cardiff

On the edge of Cardiff is this unfinished Victorian Gothic fantasy, designed in 1875 by William Burges (who also designed Cardiff Castle) for John Patrick Crichton Stuart, third Marquess of Bute, as a hunting lodge. Burges created a fairytale place with sharp, conical roofs and outrageously lavish interiors with painted ceilings and walls, sculpted and gilded figures, and elaborate furnishings.

Don't miss the clever details in the wall decoration of the drawing room – such as the painted ribbons that seem to support the family portraits, and the frog holding a bottle of cough mixture for the 'frog' in its throat.

ABOVE: THE BUTE
FAMILY ARMS.

RIGHT: CASTLE COCH'S
FAIRYTALE TOWER.

LEFT: THE ORNATE
OCTAGONAL ROOM.

CASTLE COCH
TONGWYNLAIS
CARDIFF
CF15 7JS
TEL: 029 2081 0101

Woodland

Britain claims 33 species of native trees, including the deciduous favourites such as ash, rowan, oak, beech, hawthorn and silver birch, and evergreens such as holly, Scots pine and yew.

The definition of native trees goes back to the colonisation of the countryside after the last Ice Age, before rising sea levels cut the land off from the rest of continental Europe – rendering later arrivals such the sycamore foreign interlopers.

Britain's glorious woodland is more carefully managed than might first appear. Deforestation had hit an all-time low by the beginning of the 20th century, thanks to the demands of industry. Blockades of shipping during World War II showed the weakness of relying on imported timber, and in 1919 the Forestry Commission was formed to address the needs of the country. Whole new forests were planted on purchased farmland, and the revitalisation of private enterprise was encouraged with grants, successfully reversing the trends. Meanwhile, what started as a government organisation dedicated to building and maintaining a strategic timber reserve has grown into a major body that manages more than 1 million hectares of forestry in England, Wales and Scotland, with an expanded brief to conserve wildlife and provide public amenities.

This means that much of Britain's woodland is more accessible than ever, with signed forest trails to encourage walking and cycling, information centres, and the opportunity to join in with local conservation projects.

FAR LEFT: BRITAIN'S
WOODLAND HAS
INTEREST FROM THE
SHADE-LOVING PLANTS
BELOW TO THE LEAFY
TREE CANOPY ABOVE

LEFT: AUTUMNAL
COLOUR TINTS A
HIGHLAND WOOD

Wye Valley
Welsh Borders
West of Hereford

MONMOUTH TOURIST
INFORMATION CENTRE

SHIRE HALL AGINCOURT SQUARE
MONMOUTH NP25 3DY

TEL: 01600 713899

The River Wye ends in a glorious finale as it meanders through the steep-sided wooded Wye Valley. Once busy with charcoal burning to supply local ironworks, in the late 18th century the valley became popular with romantic poets in their quest for a deeper appreciation of nature.

Monmouth town stands where the Monnow flows into the River Wye. The arcaded Shire Hall dominates the market place, Agincourt Square. Monmouth Castle was the birthplace of Henry V (1387–1422). East of the town rises the Kymin, a hill with fine views and two Georgian follies – the Naval Temple and the Round House – owned by the National Trust.

The majestic ruins of Tintern Abbey occupy a beautiful site in the Wye Valley. Though now a roofless shell as a consequence of the dissolution of the monasteries under Henry VIII, parts of the 12th- to 13th-century Cistercian abbey stand at their original height, notably the abbey church, where elaborate window tracery survives.

Guarding a vital crossing point into Wales, Chepstow Castle was built in 1067 as the invaders pushed westwards after the conquest. The stone keep is original, but the towers, walls, gatehouses and barbicans were added later. It was adapted for musketry and cannon after a long siege in the Civil War.

Ludlow
Shropshire
24 miles (39km) south of Shrewsbury

BELOW, LEFT AND RIGHT:
TWO EXAMPLES OF
THE HALF-TIMBERING
THAT IS CHARACTERISTIC
OF LUDLOW.

TOURIST INFORMATION CENTRE

CASTLE STREET
LUDLOW
SY8 1AS

TEL: 01584 875053

Georgian brickwork and earlier half-timbering grace the streets of this hilltop town, with Broad Street being a particularly harmonious example of townscape. Ludlow Castle, a border fortress begun in the late 11th century, was enlarged in the 14th century into a palace for the powerful Roger Mortimer.

Near the ancient Butter Cross, the Church of St Laurence assumes a cathedral-like grandeur, and has a fine set of 15th-century carved misericords (benches in the choir, provided for the monks to rest on during their long hours of prayer). The town has emerged as a regional gourmet capital, with an excellent range of restaurants.

The annual Ludlow Festival (June–July) involves drama and music being performed in the castle grounds.

Ironbridge Gorge Museum
Wrekin
3 miles (5km) south of Dawley

Several outstanding museums are to be found in the true birthplace of the Industrial Revolution. The Iron Bridge of 1779 did more than just span the modest River Severn – it was the first structure of its kind, and has come to symbolize the beginnings of the Industrial Revolution. In 1709 in this valley the ironmaster and engineer Abraham Darby (1678–1717) pioneered the smelting of iron ore with coke rather than charcoal, making the mass-production of metal feasible.

The Gorge is dotted with nine sites that all belong to the museum. The largest is Blists Hill Victorian Town, reconstructed on the site of an 18th-century industrial estate, with working factories, shops and workers' cottages staffed by costumed actors and craftspeople. Coalport China Museum occupies what

TOURIST INFORMATION
CENTRE

COACH ROAD
COALBROOKDALE
TF8 7DQ

TEL: 01952 432166

RIGHT: A PRINTER AT WORK IN THE BLISTS HILL MUSEUM.

BELOW, LEFT: THE IRON BRIDGE WAS A WORLD FIRST AND IS A SYMBOL OF THE INDUSTRIAL REVOLUTION.

was the Coalport China Works. Close by is the entrance to the Tar Tunnel, where you go underground to see what was a natural source of bitumen when Ironbridge was functioning. Across the river stands the Jackfield Tile Museum, within a huge Victorian tile factory that is again making decorative tiles for sale.

South of Jackfield Bridge, the Broseley Pipeworks, which used to manufacture clay tobacco pipes, has been left as it was when it closed in 1957 after 350 years of production. Beyond the Iron Bridge (which has an exhibition in its tollhouse) the Museum of the Gorge gives an overview of the development of the gorge as a whole. North of here the Coalbrookdale Museum of Iron contains the original blast furnace built by Abraham Darby, while the Darby Houses were homes to the ironmasters.

'Enginuity' is a hands-on attraction aimed at children, which invites them to try such engineering tasks as stoking a furnace.

Cirencester
Gloucestershire
14 miles (23km) northwest of Swindon

BELOW: A STROLL UP
CECILY HILL LEADS INTO
beautiful CIRENCESTER
PARK, LAID OUT IN THE
18TH CENTURY.

VISITOR INFORMATION CENTRE
THE CORN HALL
MARKET PLACE, CIRENCESTER
GL7 2NW
TEL: 01285 654180

During the Roman occupation, Cirencester was called Corinium, England's second most important city after London. Now it is a sedate market town, focusing around its Market Place, which is dominated by St John the Baptist Church, one of the grandest Cotswold 'wool churches', built when the wool trade brought great local prosperity in the 15th century.

The town's most attractive street, Cecily Hill, leads into Cirencester Park, geometrically laid out in the 18th century: there is free access for walking. The Corinium Museum celebrates the Roman heritage, with artefacts, room interiors, mosaics and murals. Craft workshops take place in the converted brewery within the Brewery Arts Centre.

Cotswolds
Gloucestershire, Warwickshire and Oxfordshire

TOURIST INFORMATION CENTRE

77 THE PROMENADE
CHELTENHAM
GL50 1PP

TEL: 01242 522878

BELOW LEFT: THE ROLLRIGHT STONES HAVE INSPIRED MUCH DEBATE ABOUT THEIR PURPOSE.

Cheltenham makes a good base for touring the beautiful Cotswolds, with its picturesque little towns and village built in the mellow honey-coloured local stone, the elegant Regency town of Cheltenham is renowned for its handsome terraces, wrought-iron balconies, leafy thoroughfares, parks, floral displays, horse racing, a music festival in July and a literature festival in October. The town spreads southwards along The Promenade, a wide, pedestrianized, leafy street with imposing statues, pavement cafés and elegant shops.

The Art Gallery and Museum in Clarence Street has an excellent section about the Arts and Crafts movement. Close by is the Holst Birthplace Museum, dedicated to Gustav Holst (1874–1934), composer of *The Planets*.

Pittville Park features lakes and a showpiece Pump Room, which dates from 1825 and is styled in the Greek Revival tradition. The Pump Room was built after a mineral spring was discovered in Pittville Park in 1715, and you can still take the salty waters here.

PAINSWICK

This town slopes to the Painswick Brook, where several former textile mills can be seen. The churchyard has 99 yews, 200 years old, clipped into arches and geometric shapes, along with 17th- and 18th-century tombstones in a range of shapes and styles. Painswick Rococo Garden is a re-creation of an 18th-century design based on a painting by Thomas Robins in 1748.

ROLLRIGHT STONES

Located near Long Compton, three groups of standing stones –
The King's Men, The King Stone and The Whispering Knights –
together span nearly 2,000 years of the Neolithic and Bronze
Ages. The King's Men is a large circle of about 70 stones.

CHARLECOTE PARK

Charlecote near Stratford-upon-Avon has been home of the
Lucy family and its forbears, the Montforts, for 900 years,
although the present rose-pink brick structure dates from 1551.
Guests have included Elizabeth I, who slept here for two nights in
1572, and the young William Shakespeare (1564–1616).

ABOVE: PRETTY
PAINSWICK IS FAMOUS
FOR THE YEW TREES IN
THE CHURCHYARD.

LEFT: THE FORMER
CARPET FACTORY BY
CHIPPING NORTON IS A
NOTABLE COTSWOLD
LANDMARK.

Stratford-upon-Avon
Warwickshire
8 miles (13km) southwest of Warwick

Before the birth of William Shakespeare, the world's greatest playwright, Stratford was a flourishing market town, where merchants built themselves imposing half-timbered houses. The details of Shakespeare's life are somewhat hazy, but the houses of his family are real enough.

Even without the Shakespeare connection, Stratford is a very appealing town on the River Avon, with many historical buildings. One of the most attractive and photogenic spots is Church Street. Most of the buildings have Georgian frontages, but the 15th-century almshouses are timber-framed, and the King Edward VI School is thought to be where Shakespeare was educated. The Guild Chapel dates from the late 15th century; it was built by Hugh Clopton, an earlier resident of the town, and is still a place of worship.

SHAKESPEARE'S BIRTHPLACE
The site most visitors head for first is in the centre of town. Whether this marks the Bard's true birthplace in 1564 is open to question, but it has become his shrine. Since his birth, this half-timbered Tudor house has changed appreciably, but the interior has been refurbished to give a good impression of the young Shakespeare's life.

ROYAL SHAKESPEARE COMPANY
The Royal Shakespeare Company (RSC) maintains Stratford's theatrical traditions, with events at its three theatres – the Royal Shakespeare Theatre, the Swan and the Other Place. The Royal Shakespeare, on Waterside, is a 1930s building and the main venue for Shakespeare's plays. The Swan occupies the site of the first Memorial Theatre, erected in 1879, destroyed in a fire in 1926 and then rebuilt.

ANNE HATHAWAY'S COTTAGE
Shakespeare's wife lived in this pretty thatched cottage. You can walk to it along the country lane from Hall's Croft to avoid the traffic. The house stayed in the Hathaway family until the 19th century, and much of the family furniture remains.

MARY ARDEN'S HOUSE AND THE SHAKESPEARE COUNTRYSIDE MUSEUM
The childhood home of Shakespeare's mother is 3 miles (5km) north of the town. The Shakespeare Countryside Museum surrounds the cottage and has displays about life and work here, as well as Glebe Farm, a working blacksmith's and a falconer.

HOLY TRINITY CHURCH

Out of town by the river is the 13th-century church where Shakespeare was baptized in 1564 and buried in 1616. His gravestone is in front of the altar.

HARVARD HOUSE

This house was the home of Katherine Rogers, mother of clergyman John Harvard (1607–38), who emigrated to Massachusetts. His generous bequests to the newly founded US college at Cambridge led to it being named after him.

NEW PLACE

The house where Shakespeare died in 1616 no longer exists, but its site is marked by a garden next to Nash's House. This was the home of Shakespeare's granddaughter's first husband.

ABOVE: BOATING PAST THE ROYAL SHAKESPEARE THEATRE ON THE RIVER AVON.

LEFT: THE THATCHED COTTAGE THAT WAS THE HOME OF SHAKESPEARE'S WIFE, ANNE HATHAWAY.

TOURIST INFORMATION CENTRE

BRIDGEFOOT
STRATFORD-UPON-
AVON
CV37 6GW

TEL: 0870 160 7930

Hidcote Manor Gardens

Gloucestershire

3 miles (5km) northeast of Chipping Camden

BELOW: TWO OF THE
ATTRACTIVE GARDEN
'ROOMS' THAT MAKE UP
HIDCOTE MANOR
GARDENS.

HIDCOTE BARTRIM
NEAR CHIPPING CAMPDEN
GL55 6LR

TEL: 01386 438333

Hidcote represents one of the great innovative garden designs, and was the creation of horticulturist Major Lawrence Johnston between 1907 and 1948. The gardens are made up of a series of structured outdoor 'rooms', each with its own character and separated by walls and hedges of copper and green beech, box, holly, hornbeam and yew. There are outstanding herbaceous borders, old roses and rare or unique plants and trees from all over the world.

The varied styles of the garden rooms peak at different times of year, making Hidcote impressive during any season. It can get overcrowded on public holidays and Sundays.

Warwick Castle
Warwickshire
9 miles (14km) southwest of Coventry

WARWICK CASTLE
WARWICK
CV34 4QU
TEL: 0870 442 2000

BELOW: WARWICK CASTLE IS STRAIGHT OUT OF A FAIRYTALE, AND MUCH ENJOYED BY VISITORS OF ALL AGES.

Warwick Castle is architecturally one of the finest examples of a medieval castle in England, with its exteriors dating back to the 14th and 15th centuries. To appreciate it from the outside, walk around the walls and through the gardens, landscaped by Capability Brown in the 1750s, with the subsequent addition of a Victorian Rose Garden and Peacock Garden. The castle is owned by the Tussaud's Group and is run as a modern tourist attraction.

The interior was thoroughly upgraded in the 17th to 19th centuries, and the private apartments are furnished as they would have been in 1898. The Royal Weekend Party uses waxwork figures to replicate aristocratic life of that time, one guest being the young Winston Churchill (1874–1965). The Kingmaker is an exhibition devoted to the castle's most significant and influential owner, Richard Neville, Earl of Warwick (1428–71). You can see Neville preparing for his final battle in 1471. Also look for the arms and armour exhibition and the eerie Dungeon and Torture Chamber.

Many visitors to the castle miss the town of Warwick itself, which was given a handsome makeover after a disastrous fire in 1694 and has some of the finest 18th-century streetscapes in England, notably in the High Street and Northgate Street. Predating the fire are two medieval gateways, the old houses in Castle Lane, the 15th-century Beauchamp tomb in the Church of St Mary, and Leycester Hospital. The latter is a wonderfully complete group of half-timbered buildings (mostly 16th-century) providing accommodation for elderly servicemen. Visitors can look into the chapel, courtyard and great hall.

Oxford
Oxfordshire
52 miles (84km) northwest of London

OXFORD INFORMATION
CENTRE

15–16 BROAD STREET
OXFORD OX1 2DA
TEL: 01865 726871

RIGHT: OXFORD'S
VERSION OF THE
'BRIDGE OF SIGHS'.

RIGHT, BELOW:
THE RADCLIFFE
CAMERA.

Enclosed by the rivers Cherwell and Thames, Oxford is a beautiful city of Cotswold stone. This historic and world-famous seat of learning is easily explored on foot. The university's colleges stand in cloistered seclusion and can be hard to identify as they are not clearly named, but between them they display a wonderful array of ancient, classical and modern architecture. Don't miss the back lanes and alleys, particularly Merton Street/Oriel Street, and Queen's Lane/New College Lane, leading beneath the Bridge of Sighs. The high street, known simply as The High, runs from Carfax Tower east to Magdalen Bridge over the River Cherwell, dividing the city into north and south.

ABOVE: PUNTS MOORED
ON THE CHERWELL AT
MAGDALEN BRIDGE.

ABOVE RIGHT:
A CEREMONIAL
PROCESSION OF DONS
ON DEGREE DAY.

CHRIST CHURCH

Founded in 1524, Oxford's largest and most visited college has the biggest quadrangle, and its chapel, Christ Church Cathedral (predating the college), is England's smallest cathedral. Within the Great Hall you will find features from the *Alice in Wonderland* stories written by former don Charles Dodgson, better known as Lewis Carroll (1832–98), while Ante Hall became Hogwarts Hall in both of the *Harry Potter* movies.

THE RIVERS THAMES AND CHERWELL

These waterways slice through remarkably verdant land close to the city centre. The tree-lined Cherwell ('charwell') provides almost rural views of Magdalen College. University rowing crews train on the Thames (also known here as the Isis). The Oxford Botanic Garden, founded in 1621, leads to Christchurch Meadow and the confluence of the rivers.

RADCLIFFE SQUARE

The architectural group found here belongs to the university. The Sheldonian Theatre (built 1664–68) was Sir Christopher Wren's first major architectural work. The Bodleian Library is one of six copyright libraries in the UK, entitled to receive a copy of every UK-published book. The circular domed Radcliffe Camera of 1737–49, by James Gibbs, is a reading room for the library.

MUSEUMS

Britain's oldest public museum (opened 1683), the Ashmolean houses Oxford University's priceless collections from the time of early man to the 20th century. The Pitt Rivers Museum has an anthropology collection of more than 250,000 objects, including masks and shrunken heads. The Museum of Oxford gives a succinct survey of the city from prehistoric times to the present.

ABOVE: THE OXFORD UNIVERSITY MUSEUM CONTAINS DINOSAURS AND OTHER EXHIBITS.

Blenheim Palace
Oxfordshire
8 miles (13km) northwest of Oxford

One of the largest private houses in Britain and the ultimate in English Baroque was designed by Sir John Vanbrugh (1664–1726) and Nicholas Hawksmoor (1661–1736); its construction was financed by Queen Anne as a gift to John Churchill, first Duke of Marlborough (1650–1722), in recognition of his crushing victory over the French at the Battle of Blenheim in 1704. It is still home of the Churchill family, now occupied by the 11th Duke and his family.

The gilded state rooms overlook lawns and formal gardens laid out by Capability Brown (1715–83). Beautiful Blenheim Lake, spanned by Vanbrugh's Grand Bridge (and it is indeed grand), forms the focal point of the grounds. From the house you can look along past the lake to a massive column, at the top of which the first duke stands surveying his empire. Also in the grounds are a butterfly house, maze, people-sized games of chess and draughts, and a wooden playground area. In addition, there is a fun miniature railway that takes you in brightly painted carriages from the house to the maze and games area.

The Churchill Exhibition is a major highlight, and is the room where Sir Winston Churchill (1874–1965), who was Britain's prime minister during World War II, was born on 30 November. He is buried, with his wife, in the village of Bladon nearby.

ABOVE: THE FORMAL GARDENS CONTAIN MANY STATUESQUE ORNAMENTS.

LEFT: REFLECTIONS OF BLENHEIM PALACE — THE STATE ROOMS, VIEWED ACROSS THE FORMAL GARDENS.

BLENHEIM PALACE

WOODSTOCK
OX20 1PX

TEL: 01993 811325
(RECORDING):
08700 602080

Audley End
Essex
1 mile (1.5km) west of Saffron Walden

BELOW, LEFT: THE GREAT HALL IS A SUPERB EXAMPLE OF A GRAND JACOBEAN COUNTRY MANSION.

BELOW, RIGHT: AUDLEY END WAS BUILT FOR THE LORD TREASURER, LATER FOUND GUILTY OF EMBEZZLEMENT.

AUDLEY END
SAFFRON WALDEN
CB11 4JF
TEL: 01799 522399

One of England's greatest Jacobean country houses lies just west of Saffron Walden. Built between 1605 and 1614 by Thomas Howard, first Earl of Suffolk, on the scale of a great royal palace, it was reduced in size over the next century, with modifications by architects Sir John Vanbrugh (1664–1726) and Robert Adam (1728–92). James I – possibly in a fit of envious pique – decided it was 'too large for a king'.

The interior is largely the influence of the third Baron Braybrooke, who inherited the house in 1825 and filled the many rooms (30 are now open to the public) with furnishings and a collection of art.

The gardens and parkland that surround the house were landscaped by Capability Brown (1715–83), with Palladian bridges and temples.

The nearby busy medieval market town of Saffron Walden, which was named after the saffron crocus growing in local fields, makes a good detour for its timber-framed buildings, turf maze and grand church.

Cambridge

Cambridgeshire

49 miles (79km) north of London

Modern industry may be the first sight of Cambridge as you enter from the flat countryside that surrounds it, so the incongruously beautiful core of this historic city may be a very nice surprise. About half of the university's 30 or so colleges have medieval origins, and are mainly within 10 minutes' walk of each other. You can visit most of them, although some charge an entrance fee, and many are closed during the time of exams.

LEFT: SUPERB FAN-VAULTING IN THE CHAPEL OF KING'S COLLEGE

BELOW: THE CHAPEL FORMS ONE SIDE OF A TRANQUIL COURTYARD

The obvious starting point is King's Parade; climb the tower of the University Church (also known as Great St Mary's) for a rare high-level view. On one side is the classical Senate House, where university students receive their degrees, next to Gonville and Caius College (pronounced 'keys' – and everyone drops the Gonville part). In the other direction, Market Hill, a hill only in name, is the venue for a bustling market.

Don't miss the King's College Chapel, known throughout Britain for its Chapel Choir. It's well worth catching a choral evensong. The chapel was built between 1446 and 1515 under Henry VI (1421–71), Henry VII (1457–1509) and Henry VIII (1491–1547). It is perhaps the greatest example of the uniquely

RIGHT: PUNTING ALONG THE BACKS OF THE COLLEGES IS A FAVOURITE PASTIME FOR STUDENTS AND VISITORS.

LEFT: THE GOTHIC GATE TO KING'S COLLEGE.

RIGHT: INTERIOR OF THE FITZWILLIAM MUSEUM.

English late Gothic Perpendicular style, typified by its wedding-cake fan-vaulting that made it the largest single-span vaulted roof of its time. By the altar is Peter Paul Rubens' masterpiece *The Adoration of the Magi*, donated anonymously in 1962.

Trinity is the largest college in Cambridge, founded in 1546 by Henry VIII, and its Great Court is the largest of the courtyards at both Cambridge and Oxford universities. One of Trinity's other major features is the Wren Library, which houses almost 60,000 historic books and manuscripts, including the original manuscript of *Winnie-the-Pooh* by A. A. Milne (a Trinity student). The second largest college is St John's, founded in 1511. Its features include the turreted gatehouse and the Bridge of Sighs.

The best of the rest of the colleges include Queens'; Emmanuel's garden; Jesus, with cloister-like seclusion and an impressive chapel; and Clare, an elegant Renaissance creation.

Two of Cambridge's best museums are free: the Fitzwilliam Museum, with its fine art including works by Cézanne, Picasso and Constable; and stylish Kettle's Yard, offering more avant-garde art.

TOURIST INFORMATION CENTRE
THE OLD LIBRARY
WHEELER STREET
CB2 3QB

TEL: 0906 586 2526

Norfolk Broads
Northeast Norfolk

Between Norwich and the North Sea coast lie the Broads, a complex of six slow-moving rivers and 41 broads (shallow lakes), providing 122 miles (196km) of navigable waterways. Formed by peat digging in medieval times, this is Britain's largest nationally protected wetland, and the natural habitat of many rare plants and animals. Hiking, angling and birdwatching are all popular activities in the area, but the best way to see the Broads is by boat. The focus of activity is the small, busy town of Wroxham, 8 miles (13km) northeast of Norwich, where boats can be hired.

BROADS INFORMATION CENTRE

STATION ROAD
HOVETON NR12 8UR

TEL: 01603 610734 (WINTER);
01603 782281 (APRIL-OCT)

RIGHT AND BELOW:
WINDMILLS ARE AN EYE-
CATCHING FEATURE OF
THE NORFOLK BROADS.

Southwold

Suffolk

4 miles (6km) east of Blythburgh

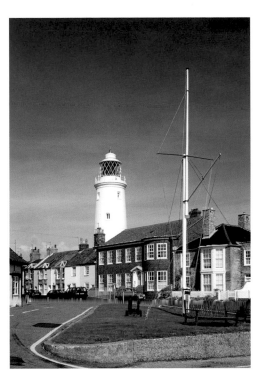

TOURIST INFORMATION
CENTRE

69 HIGH STREET
SOUTHWOLD
IP18 6DS

TEL: 01502 724729

The allure of this port-turned-resort is its sedate, old-fashioned character. Groups of brick and colour-washed cottages cluster around greens beneath three landmarks: the lighthouse, Adnam's brewery and the soaring tower of Perpendicular-style St Edmund's Church.

In the town centre are art galleries, antiques shops, tea rooms and pubs, most selling the highly esteemed Adnam's ales. Below the Sailors' Reading Room – a social club for mariners, with a local history display – some 200 colourful beach huts dating from the early 1900s line the beach.

LEFT: THE ATTRACTIVE TOWN OF SOUTHWOLD, WITH ITS LANDMARK LIGHTHOUSE TOWERING IN THE BACKGROUND.

BELOW: THE EPITOME OF THE BRITISH SEASIDE – A ROW OF BEACH HUTS ON THE SHORE AT SOUTHWOLD.

Liverpool

Liverpool

178 miles (287km) northwest of London

TOURIST INFORMATION
CENTRE

ATLANTIC PAVILION
ALBERT DOCK
LIVERPOOL L3 4EA

TEL: 0151 709 5111

RIGHT: A ROOFTOP
'LIVER BIRD'.

BELOW: THE ROYAL
LIVER BUILDING (1911),
ONE OF LIVERPOOL'S
MAIN LANDMARKS.

Its days as one of the great ports of the British Empire have long gone, but the grandeur of its architecture echoes the boom years – Liverpool has more landmark buildings than any English city outside London.

From Lime Street Station, walk past neoclassical St George's Hall (1854), along Dale Street and Water Street to the waterfront. Here is the Royal Liver Building, with the famous sculptural Liver Birds perched high on the towers. Albert Dock (1846) was restored in 1988 into gift shops, cafés and major museums. Dedicated fans will visit the Beatles Story – there's a mock-up of The Cavern club, the white piano on which John Lennon (1940–80) composed 'Imagine' (1971), and other memorabilia.

At either end of Hope Street are the two cathedrals. The vast, sandstone Anglican Liverpool Cathedral, designed by Giles Gilbert Scott, was started in 1904 and inaugurated in 1978. The concrete Metropolitan Cathedral (Roman Catholic) was built in 1967 and is known as the Mersey Funnel. It was designed by Frederick Gibberd and is brilliantly lit by blue stained glass.

The Walker Art Gallery houses one of the UK's best provincial art collections, including works by local artist George Stubbs (1724–1806), noted for his paintings of horses. The Maritime Museum, in Albert Dock, gives an insight into the city's maritime past. Next door, Tate Liverpool houses an excellent collection of modern art. At the Museum of Liverpool Life, you can learn more about what makes the city tick.

From Albert Dock, the Magical Mystery Tour goes to Strawberry Fields, Penny Lane and the childhood homes of John Lennon (Mendips on Menlove Avenue, a 1930s semi) and Sir Paul McCartney (20 Forthlin Road, a 1950s house where he often rehearsed with the rest of the group). Both houses are now owned by the National Trust.

Chester

Cheshire

34 miles (55km) southwest of Manchester

First a Roman city called Deva, then a medieval port and cathedral city, and then, after the River Dee silted up, a place where prosperous Georgian merchants settled – Chester has many layers of history. It has the most complete medieval city walls in Britain encompassing the entire centre. You can walk along or beside them to get an excellent overview of the city. One of the original city gateways is Eastgate, surmounted by a highly ornate clock dating from 1897; just to the south, the wall passes the partly excavated site of the largest Roman amphitheatre in the country, and close by the Roman Garden has re-erected Roman columns.

The best Roman remains are in the Grosvenor Museum, with Roman tombstones and other displays on the city's history. The Deva Roman Experience replicates the sights, sounds and smells of the Roman settlement.

Central Chester is a crossing of two main streets (both largely traffic-free): along these run the Rows, two tiers of arcaded shopping streets, one above the other. The scheme dates from medieval times and is unique in Britain. The black-and-white buildings at The Cross are 19th-century Tudor replications, but Chester has many original examples of half-timbered architecture. To the north is Chester Cathedral, part of the most complete medieval monastic complex in Britain. Although heavily restored, it has retained beautiful carved 13th-century choir stalls.

CHESTER VISITOR CENTRE

VICAR'S LANE
CHESTER CH1 1QX

TEL: 01244 402111

RIGHT: CHESTER IS WELL KNOWN FOR THE ROWS, ITS TWO-TIER ARCADED SHOPPING STREETS.

Blackpool

Blackpool
15 miles (24km) west of Preston

What Blackpool does, it does extremely well: donkey rides, amusement arcades and big rides. During the 19th century, local factory workers traditionally came here for their annual week's holiday to enjoy the famous promenade, the long sandy beach and the theatres.

There can be few better-known landmarks than Blackpool Tower, which is, in fact, a scale copy of Paris's famous Eiffel Tower. The Blackpool version is, however, more than just a tower. It rises 519ft (158m) out of a building that is large enough to accommodate the famous circus and the vast Tower Ballroom, with its mighty Wurlitzer organ. There are lifts to the top of the tower, from where there are magnificent views over the resort of Blackpool itself and the miles of coastline that surround it.

Brash, brazen and bustling, Blackpool wears its heart on its sleeve. The Pleasure Beach is still the main draw for visitors to Blackpool and is one of the most visited amusement parks in England. Four of the original wooden roller-coasters remain, along with many other rides. The original Big Dipper was opened here in 1923 and is still going strong, rivalled today by the world's biggest rollercoaster, The Big One. There is nothing subtle about the attractions of Pleasure Beach. Those who want their pleasures to involve 'white knuckles' will not be disappointed.

The best time to visit Blackpool is in the autumn. At a time when most other resorts are putting up the shutters at the end of the season, Blackpool gears up for the annual influx of visitors who come to see the famous Illuminations – huge moving tableaux of fairytales and brilliantly lit trams. Running 7 miles (11km) along the seafront, the Illuminations bring a touch of the glamour and sparkle of Las Vegas to the country's biggest holiday resort. A leisurely tram ride along the front is one of the best ways of viewing the Illuminations.

LEFT AND FAR LEFT: OVER-THE-TOP ILLUMINATIONS AND DONKEY RIDES ARE THE ESSENCE OF BLACKPOOL.

BLACKPOOL TOURISM
1 CLIFTON ST
BLACKPOOL FY1 1LY
TEL: 01253 478222

ABOVE: THE 19TH-CENTURY BLACKPOOL TOWER, A SCALED-DOWN VERSION OF THE EIFFEL TOWER IN PARIS.

Yorkshire Dales National Park

North Yorkshire

The Yorkshire Dales represent some of the most enticing terrain of the Pennine Hills, the backbone of northern England. Below the bleak gritstone moors runs a series of limestone valleys (dales), each with its own subtle character.

The villages, built of stone and often ranged around greens, are very much part of the landscape, and many grew up around the now-vanished lead industry in the boom years of the 18th and 19th centuries.

Corridor-like Wharfedale runs from Bolton Abbey, with its ruined 12th-century priory beside the still-functioning priory church, past the mini-gorge of The Strid, the bustling village of Grassington and the overhang of Kilnsey Crag.

Further north, the scenery is more mellow and expansive in Wensleydale, a valley renowned for its waterfalls, the crumbly Wensleydale cheese and the forbidding ruins of Middleham and Bolton Castle. Swaledale is a remote and secretive place studded with stone barns and relics of lead-mining, and with the fast-flowing River Swale linking Reeth, with its charming sloping green, and the market town of Richmond.

To the west are the Yorkshire Dales' most spectacular limestone landscapes, including the Three Peaks (the three highest hills – Whernside, Ingleborough and Pen-y-Ghent). North of Malham is Malham Cove, a limestone cliff beneath a deep-fissured limestone pavement. To the east, Gordale Scar was formed when a cavern collapsed, leaving a gorge shadowed by huge formidable crags.

At the northwestern extremity of the national park, the Howgill Hills provide a great contrast, as they are formed by high, rounded fells of slate. There are stern hikes over them, but the walk up the relatively modest summit of Winder from the town of Sedbergh provides a good taste.

YORKSHIRE DALES
NATIONAL PARK
AUTHORITY

COLVEND
HEBDEN ROAD
GRASSINGTON
SKIPTON
BD23 5LB

TEL: 01756 752748

LEFT: THE MIDDLE FALLS AT AYSGARTH FALLS.

ABOVE: THE UNSPOILT VILLAGE OF ASKRIGG LIES IN WENSLEYDALE.

RIGHT: THE DENT HEAD VIADUCT CARRIES THE SETTLE-CARLISLE RAILWAY LINE OVER THE YORKSHIRE DALES.

Haworth

Bradford

2 miles (3km) southwest of Keighley

When Haworth was home to the Brontë family in the 19th century, it was still a textile-manufacturing village. The steep, cobbled streets are surrounded by wild moorland, and the look of the village has changed little since the Brontës lived here, despite the gift shops and tea rooms.

Haworth became home to the Brontës in 1820 when Patrick Brontë (1777–1861) was appointed its rector. It was while living at the Parsonage here that the three Brontë sisters – Charlotte (1816–55), Emily (1818–48) and Anne (1820–49) – wrote their most famous novels, respectively *Jane Eyre* (1847), *Wuthering Heights* (1847) and *The Tenant of Wildfell Hall* (1848). You can follow well-trodden paths past the Brontë Falls to the ruins of Top Withins farmhouse, reputedly the model for nature-loving Emily's *Wuthering Heights*.

The Parsonage sits at the top of Main Street, overlooking the church. Built in 1778, it has been restored to how it would have looked in the Brontës' day. Mementoes include the children's handwritten miniature books, the sofa on which Emily died and Charlotte's wedding bonnet. You can also visit the Brontë Weaving Shed, on North Street, where you can see traditional 19th-century commemorative Brontë Tweed being made.

Steam trains from Keighley run by the Keighley and Worth Valley Railway are a good way to get to the village.

LEFT: THE BRONTË FAMILY HOME HAS BEEN RESTORED AND IS NOW A MUSEUM.

ABOVE: HAWORTH LIES ABOVE THE MOORS THAT GAVE GREAT INSPIRATION TO EMILY BRONTË.

TOURIST INFORMATION CENTRE

2–4 WEST LANE HAWORTH BD22 8EF

TEL: 01535 642329

Fountains Abbey
North Yorkshire
2 miles (3km) west of Ripon

Ripon
Near Harrogate
HG4 3DY
Tel: 01765 608888

BELOW: FOUNTAINS ABBEY, ONCE WEALTHY AND POWERFUL, IS NOW JUST A RUIN.

Heart-stopping vistas greet visitors to Britain's most complete monastic ruins, with a medieval deer park and elegant 18th-century water gardens.

Fountains Abbey was established in 1132 by 13 monks seeking a simple life, and this damp, rocky, desolate ravine fitted the bill perfectly, with a supply of stone and timber for building, shelter from the rough northern weather, and an abundance of spring water. The abbey became extremely wealthy, but was closed down by Henry VIII during his dissolution of the country's monasteries in 1539. Yet it has survived as Britain's largest abbey ruin and you can still see the church tower, dating from around 1500, soaring above the Norman nave. Wander too among the remains of the monastic quarters and into the vaulted cellarium.

The later owners beautified the estate and it was sold to Sir Stephen Proctor, who commissioned the building of Fountains Hall (1598–1604), partly with stone taken from the abbey.

Portmeirion
One Man's Fantasy

Creating Portmeirion In 1925, Clough Williams-Ellis bought an overgrown finger of land at the base of the Llyn Peninsula. In its day, this had been occupied by two castles – Deudraeth and Aber Iau – as well as a foundry, a shipyard and some cottages. But it had since been abandoned, and the neglected site provided Clough, already a distinguished architect, with the perfect opportunity to realise a cherished dream.

Clough William-Ellis was one of those who, in the early 20th century, became preoccupied with the need to combine function with aesthetic beauty. Portmeirion was a chance to put his own theories into practice. Here, he would prove that a new development need not ruin its surroundings; he would reconstruct 'fallen buildings' rescued from demolition, and give his own architectural imagination free rein. Between 1925 and 1976 the project evolved, staying true to Clough's motto: 'Cherish the past, adorn the present, construct for the future.'

A 1920s Oddity Portmeirion is the embodiment of one man's ideas and, in many ways, the embodiment of an age. It was begun in the inter-war years, when Britain was caught between economic difficulty and post-war euphoria. Thousands of soldiers had returned from the trenches in 1918 to find themselves out of work; no new homes had been built during the hostilities, and there was an acute shortage of housing. At the same time, in the face of urban expansion, many began to fear for the survival of the countryside, which seemed all the more precious and vulnerable after four years of global warfare. These concerns all played a part in Clough Williams-Ellis's career. He became involved with the housing movement, taking up a challenge, issued by the editor (his future father-in-law) of The Spectator, to design affordable rural accommodation. He was also a tireless campaigner for conservation, helping to found the Council for the Protection of Rural England in 1926 and the Campaign for the Protection of Rural Wales in 1928. The natural landscape was an essential part of his plans for

LEFT: THE FABULOUS ITALIANATE VILLAGE, GARDENS AND ORNAMENTAL POND AT PORTMEIRION.

RIGHT: CLASSICAL STYLE STATUE OF ATLAS SET IN THE GARDENS.

RIGHT, NEXT PAGE: VIEW ACROSS THE ESTUARY FROM PORTMEIRION.

Portmeirion, and for all its eccentricity, the village still sits in perfect harmony with the surrounding wooded hills and coastal scenery.

As well as being an experiment in town planning, Portmeirion was a splash of colour in a world made bleak by war. Clough's intention was always to give everyone 'a taste of lavishness, gaiety and cultivated design'. Its strange and wonderful mixture of styles brings together Arts and Crafts, Palladian, baroque, Eastern mystic and fantastic. A year after its completion in 1965, television cameras moved in to film the cult fantasy-mystery series *The Prisoner*.

A walk around a bizarre Italianate village

❶ The walk begins with a circuit around the village itself, reached past two pink Palladian tollbooths, where you pay your admission fee (which funds the upkeep of the village and grounds). Follow the path under the arch of the Gatehouse, with its painted ceiling, and then of the Classical Bridge House, and pass Toll House, a weatherboarded building decorated with bells, signs and a painted statue of St Peter. To the left is the Battery, and behind that the Italian-style bell tower, partly built with stones from Deudraeth Castle. On the right is the Pantheon, or Dome; beneath it, a painted loggia houses a gilt Buddha. The path continues to the central Piazza, with its fabulous arrangement of pool, fountain, gloriette, Gothic pavilion and columns bearing Burmese dancers.

❷ Throughout the walk, as it leads round the village and out to the headland gardens, there are unexpected touches and embellishments – a painted mermaid; intertwined dolphins; a bust of Shakespeare; a stone lion. Walking through this Snowdonia landscape is like stepping into the elaborate escapism of a Hollywood set.

❸ Having left the village itself past Fountain, the house where Noël Coward wrote Blithe Spirit in 1941, and the Portmeirion Hotel, the route leads round the headland, passing the Observatory Tower with its figure of Nelson, on the way to the Lighthouse, at Portmeirion's southernmost point. You soon reach a left-hand track to a viewpoint above White Sands Bay; after enjoying the sea view, return to the main route and continue to the Ghost Garden, named after the whispering of the wind through the eucalyptus leaves. You now turn back towards the village, passing the June-flowering rhododendrons before re-entering the site past Salutation, originally a stable block and now housing a shop selling Portmeirion pottery, designed by Clough's daughter, Susan.

Distance: 3 miles (4.8km)

Total ascent: 150ft (46m)

Paths: surfaced paths, woodland tracks: can be muddy and slippery

Terrain: village streets, cliff path, woods, stone steps

Gradients: some steep climbs in the gardens

Refreshments: Cadwallader's ice-cream parlour

Park: car park near entrance to village

OS Map: OS Outdoor Leisure 18 Snowdonia – Harlech, Porthmadog & Baal

Peak District National Park
Derbyshire

BELOW, LEFT: A NARROW PATH MEANDERS THROUGH CAVE DALE. BELOW: PEAK CAVERN WINDS DEEPER INTO THE GROUND.

BAKEWELL INFORMATION CENTRE
OLD MARKET HALL
BRIDGE STREET
BAKEWELL DE45 1DS
TEL: 01629 813227

Ringed by industrial cities such as Manchester and Sheffield, the Peak District has been given the status of a national park and provides an exhilarating sense of freedom and space away from the industry.

The Peak District is really two landscapes: the Dark Peak is an area of bleak, open gritstone moors with dramatic rocky edges, such as Stanage Edge, while the White Peak is formed of classic limestone country with stone-walled pastures cut by deep dales (valleys), such as Dovedale, Lathkill Dale and Monsal Dale.

The area's many villages include Tissington, with wide grassy borders and a Jacobean hall, and Eyam, the village that, finding itself ravaged by plague in 1665, deliberately isolated itself from the outside world. The canalside village of Cromford had the world's first water-powered mill in 1771, now a museum.

The ruins of Peveril Castle overlook Castleton at the heart of the Peak's cave district, with several caverns open to the public, including the Blue John Cavern, with its vast stalactite- and stalagmite-covered interior. Also worth visiting in the area are Buxton, Chatsworth House, Haddon Hall, and Lyme Park.

Chatsworth House
Derbyshire
7 miles (11km) northwest of Matlock

CHATSWORTH
BAKEWELL
DE45 1PP
TEL: 01246 565300

BELOW: CHATSWORTH HOUSE IS APPROACHED VIA A BRIDGE OVER THE RIVER DERWENT.

This palatial home of the Duke and Duchess of Devonshire is set in the Peak District. The original house dates from 1551, but most of what you see was built between 1686 and 1707. The Painted Hall is magnificently baroque, with marble floors, a painted ceiling and a spectacular staircase. Among the 30 rooms on show are the State Bedroom, where George II (1683–1760) died. George V (1865–1936) and Queen Mary slept in this room when they visited Chatsworth in 1933. Among the great works of art spread throughout the house are works by Antonio Canova, Rembrandt van Rijn, Paolo Veronese and Tintoretto. The library contains about 17,000 books.

The 18th-century landscaper Capability Brown laid out the park, and in the 19th century Joseph Paxton (1803–65) was head gardener before he went on to design the Crystal Palace near London for the Great Exhibition of 1851.

There is plenty to explore in the estate, including a cottage garden, a kitchen garden, an excellent farm shop, a maze, 5 miles (8km) of paths leading past rare trees and shrubs, ponds, artful fountains and outdoor sculptures. Perhaps the most memorable feature outside is the 656-ft (200-m) water cascade. It was designed in 1696, with every step of the stone slope built slightly differently to vary the sound that the water makes.

Lake District
Cumbria

TOURIST INFORMATION
CENTRE

VICTORIA STREET
WINDERMERE
LA23 IAD

TEL: 015394 46499

BOTTOM LEFT: RYDAL MOUNT AND GARDENS, THE HOME OF WILLIAM WORDSWORTH FROM 1813. BOTTOM RIGHT: INSPIRING REFLECTIONS OF CAUSEY PIKE IN DERWENT WATER, CALF CLOSE BAY.

Variously known as the Lake District, Lakeland or just The Lakes, this is an extraordinarily diverse area of mountains and lakes tucked into England's northwest corner. There's a wide choice of walking routes, from the high summits of Scafell Pike and Helvellyn to strolls through tranquil valleys and along lake shores. Or you can see it on a cruise – options include the Victorian steam yacht *Gondola* for a trip on Coniston Water, or a lake steamer on Ullswater, overlooking the waterfall Aira Force.

Fortunately there's also a range of indoor attractions for the many inclement days, including visits to the houses of the area's most famous residents. Among them are Hill Top, home of children's author Beatrix Potter (1866–1943), and Rydal Mount, home of poet William Wordsworth (1770–1850) from 1813 until his death. He and his wife Dorothy lived at Dove Cottage in Grasmere, and Brantwood was the home of artist and social critic John Ruskin (1819–1900).

WINDERMERE
The Lake District resorts of Windermere and Bowness merge together on the east shore of Lake Windermere, England's longest lake (10.5 miles/17km). For most visitors, the lake and its villa-speckled wooded shores itself are of prime interest.

Just north of Bowness, the Windermere Steamboat Museum has restored historic craft on display and also offers boat trips on the lake.

TOWNEND
Townend has no electricity, and epitomizes the remoteness of the Lake District in centuries past. It remained the property of the farming Browne family for over 300 years until it was taken over by the National Trust in 1943. The mainly 17th-century house has the Brownes' hand-carved furniture and domestic implements, with a downhouse for washing, cooking, pickling and brewing, and a firehouse with living quarters.

KESWICK
Keswick's position on Derwent Water is the key to its appeal as the major resort in the northern Lake District. Walkers venture from here all year round to the summit of Skiddaw, into the crag-lined valley of Borrowdale or along the gentle waterside paths by the lake. The Keswick Launch connects points around the lake – a round-trip ticket lets you hop on and off as you please. You can learn about the town's history of pencil-making at the Cumberland Pencil Museum, just west of the town.

KENDAL
For 600 years up to the 19th century, this town also flourished as a milling town. Today, although the manufacturing industries have dwindled, Kendal still possesses many former weavers' yards as well as numerous ginnels (alleyways), mostly to be found just off Highgate and Stricklandgate.

Hadrian's Wall
Northumberland

Northumbria preserves the best section of Hadrian's Wall, Britain's longest and most spectacular Roman remains. Once 76 miles (120km) long, the wall was built AD122–28 by the Roman Emperor Hadrian (AD76–138) to control trade over the border, rather than to keep out the barbarians to the north. The B6318 road, which runs parallel for part of the way, follows the line of the Roman military way that served the regular forts and observation turrets along the wall. A deep defensive ditch – the vallum – was dug later on the south side of the wall.

The finest preserved sections are between Chollerford in the east and Haltwhistle in the west. At Housesteads Roman Fort the latrines have seating for 12 soldiers. Close to here is Vindolanda Fort, with reconstructions of part of the wall and buildings, and a museum displaying local excavations.

Chesters Roman Fort, a cavalry fort, has the remains of the bathhouse, headquarters and barracks. Corbridge Roman Site was the supply base for the Roman invasion of Scotland in AD80, with some well-preserved granaries.

For an idea of Roman-style bathing, visit the reconstructed bathhouse at Segedunum Roman Fort at Wallsend. A 115ft (35m) tower gives a superb view of the remains of the fort itself. At South Shields, Arbeia Roman Fort has a reconstructed gatehouse and recreated scenes of life in the camp. At the wall's west end, the finest monument is Birdoswald Fort, where the west gate, drill hall and granary buildings have been excavated.

At Carrawburgh are the atmospheric remains of the Mithraic Temple, a place of worship for the soldiers, dedicated to the god Mithras. Newcastle's Museum of Antiquities has a reconstruction.

ABOVE: EXCAVATIONS HAVE REVEALED THE GARRISON'S FORTS AND LIVING QUARTERS.

LEFT: SECTIONS OF THE WALL CAN STILL BE SEEN STRETCHING ACROSS THE LANDSCAPE.

TOURIST INFORMATION CENTRE

WENTWORTH CAR PARK
HEXHAM
NE46 1QE

TEL: 01434 652220

Durham

Durham

14 miles (23km) south of Newcastle

Durham is a World Heritage Site with a magnificent cathedral and captivating views. The mighty three-towered cathedral, built mostly over 40 years from 1093, stands high on the cliff above the River Wear. During its construction, the pointed Gothic arch came into use, and the transition from the rounded Norman arch is visible within the nave. Huge cylindrical pillars are carved with geometric designs

The Galilee Chapel at the west end is decorated with carved zigzags, giving a jazzy setting for the tomb of the Venerable Bede (c673–735), Britain's first historian. At the east end lies the body of St Cuthbert, one of the region's major saints. The Bishop's throne is the most elevated in Britain – fittingly, for Durham's Prince-Bishops were a law unto themselves, and even the king needed permission to enter their lands. The cloisters and precincts represent the most complete survival of a medieval monastery in England; off the cloister, the Treasury has relics of St Cuthbert and treasures that belonged to the Prince-Bishops.

On the opposite end of the hilltop is the Norman castle, whose great circular keep contains the Gallery and Chapel, as well as the medieval Great Hall and an ornate 17th-century staircase. There is also a series of 18th-century state rooms, where the Prince-Bishops held court. Since 1832, when the Bishops gave up their powers and moved out, it has been one of the colleges of prestigious Durham University.

TOURIST INFORMATION CENTRE

MILLENNIUM PLACE
DURHAM
DH1 1WA

TEL: 0191 384 3720

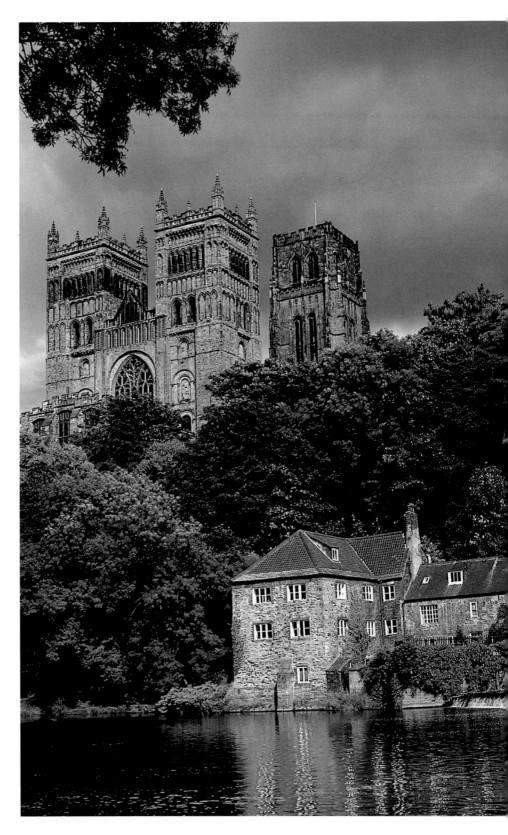

RIGHT: DURHAM CATHEDRAL'S TOWERS ARE VISIBLE THROUGH TREES LOOMING OVER FULLER MILL.

York

York

212 miles (341km) north of London

This strikingly beautiful city straddling the River Ouse is one of Britain's premier sights. York has a multitude of museums and buildings spanning a range of historic periods. Much of the city's compact centre is pedestrianized, so it is a great place to explore on foot. Among some of the most evocative streets are The Shambles, originally a street of butchers' shops and retaining overhanging, jettied, timber-framed buildings, and Stonegate, where shop signs and frontages span several centuries. You should also look for York's distinguished clutch of medieval churches. Arguably the finest is Holy Trinity (Goodramgate).

York was founded by the Roman army in AD71 as the town of Eboracum. A few remains of the original settlement are to be

TOURIST INFORMATION
BUREAU

20 GEORGE HUDSON
STREET
YORK
YO1 6WR

TEL: 01904 554455

LEFT: THIS ROMAN COLUMN DATING FROM THE 4TH CENTURY WAS RE-ERECTED IN MINSTER YARD IN 1971.

PREVIOUS PAGE: THE MAGNIFICENT MEDIEVAL YORK MINSTER AND THE SHAMBLES IN YORK.

seen above ground, such as the walls of the old fortress in the foundations of York Minster. After the Romans left, Viking settlers took over, and the town became Jorvik. They also established the city's gateways and named the streets, many of them on the Roman lines. In the Middle Ages, York flourished as a trading city, and the walls that were started in Roman times were rebuilt, taking in a larger area both sides of the River Ouse.

YORK MINSTER

Dating from 1220–1472, this is Europe's largest Gothic cathedral north of the Alps, with two towers, richly traceried windows and a huge west front. Look particularly for the Five Sisters (a quintet of lancet windows), and for the depictions of Genesis and Revelation in the east window of c1250 – the world's largest area of medieval stained glass within a single window.

CITY WALL

York is enclosed by a virtually complete wall, pierced by bars (gateways). Monk Bar houses the Richard III Museum, presenting the story of the Monarch (1452–85) portrayed by Shakespeare as a murderer, and enabling you to reach your own verdict.

MUSEUMS

The displays in the York Castle Museum include some full-size reproductions of Victorian and Edwardian shopping streets. The Jorvik Viking Centre, on the other hand, offers visitors a unique journey back to York in the 10th century.

ABOVE: THE RUINOUS REMAINS NORMAN ST MARY'S ABBEY.

North York Moors National Park
North Yorkshire

Though not the highest nor the most ruggedly dramatic of the national parks, this is a highly distinctive corner of England. Medieval stone crosses, placed as waymarkers, punctuate the bare waste of the moors, which feature the country's largest continuous tract of heather – a spectacular purple carpet in late summer. There's an exhilarating sense of solitude up here among the skylarks and grouse.

Below are a series of lush, green dales (valleys) such as Esk Dale and Rosedale, each with trademark attractive villages such as Hutton-le-Hole and Coxwold that sport red-tiled roofs, yellowstone walls and spacious village greens. (Come off-season if you want to experience them without everyone else.)

The quiet market town of Helmsley, on the park's southern edge, makes a useful base for the area, and has the jagged ruins of a 13th-century castle to explore.

Coastal attractions include a range of formidable sandstone cliffs and a number of impossibly squashed-together fishing villages such as Robin Hood's Bay, with a smuggling history to rival any other, and Staithes, which has maintained some of its traditional qualities.

You can get a good idea of the landscape by driving or cycling along the many quiet roads, or from the steam and diesel trains on the North Yorkshire Moors Railway. But the best views of all are from the long-distance walker's route, the Cleveland Way, as it snakes along the escarpments, taking in the huge inland cliff of Sutton Bank, the mini-summit of Roseberry Topping and the entire coastal stretch from Saltburn-by-the-Sea to Filey.

Early Christians left some impressive monuments, including the monastic remains of 14th-century Mount Grace Priory, 11 miles (18km) north of Thirsk, where a silent order of monks once lived, 12th-century Byland Abbey near Coxwold, and Rievaulx Abbey.

ABOVE: THE VIEW OVER
OPEN HEATHLAND FROM
BLAKEYS RIDGE.

LEFT: YOUNG RALPH'S
CROSS, THE NP EMBLEM.

TOURIST INFORMATION CENTRE
NORTH YORK MOORS NATIONAL PARK
THE OLD VICARAGE
BONDGATE
HELMSLEY
YORK YO62 5BP

TEL: 01439 770657

Whitby
North Yorkshire
17 miles (27km) northwest of Scarborough

Whitby is a blend of fishing port and Victorian seaside resort, set along the slopes of the deep valley of the River Esk. Prominent among the boats that pack the harbour are the traditional flat-bottomed fishing cobles.

The 13th-century ruins of Whitby Abbey are reached by 199 steps. The visitor centre gives a vivid audiovisual guide from the days of its 7th-century founder, St Hilda, to its shelling by German warships in World War I. The abbey, steps and graveyard of St Mary's Church feature in Bram Stoker's novel *Dracula* (1897).

A statue of the great explorer Captain James Cook (1728–79) looks over the town from the West Cliff. He was born close by in Marton and his ships were built at Whitby; the Captain Cook Memorial Museum in Grape Lane tells the story of his life and voyages of discovery.

Whitby provides a good base for visiting the North York Moors and coast. Three extraordinarily built fishing villages are located near the town. Staithes has escaped prettification and is set along a narrow, steep-sided creek, often bearing the brunt of storms and floods. A 20-minute clifftop walk leads to the village from Runswick Bay, smaller and neater, tightly packed beneath the cliff. Further south, Robin Hood's Bay was rife with smuggling in the 18th century. It hugs a steep slope, and is densely packed with red pantiled roofs, tiny alleys and crooked lanes. From here there are breezy walks south along the highest cliffs on England's east coast.

Don't miss Whitby Museum in Pannett Park. It offers an idiosyncratic collection of fossils, natural history and Whitby jet as well as seafaring memorabilia.

TOURIST INFORMATION
CENTRE

LANGBOURNE ROAD
WHITBY YO21 1YN

TEL: 01947 602674

LEFT: THE REMAINS OF WHITBY ABBEY LOOM ABOVE THE TOWN.

RIGHT: THE FORMER WHALING PORT OF WHITBY WAS HOME TO EXPLORER JAMES COOK.

Bridges

There is a fascination about bridges, which has as much to do with an apparent defiance of space and gravity as a fascinating exposure of function in form.

Since trees could be laid across a stream, the earliest form of simple beam bridges have existed. Naturally, the earliest ones that survive into this modern age are those made out of great slabs of stone, such as those found along the ancient packhorse routes on Dartmoor.

Beam bridges are limited by the length of the available raw material, and when longer structures were required, the development of the stone arch began. These structures developed from the single high arch such as that seen at Wycoller, North Yorkshire — just wide enough for a single horse to cross if led carefully — to the superb multiple-arched structures of stone and brick that span across the country. William Adam's graceful bridge at Aberfeldy (1733) and the striding Ribble Viaduct (1838) are notable examples.

Isambard Kingdom Brunel's Clifton Suspension Bridge, 75m (245ft) above the Avon Gorge near Bristol, was one of the first of its kind in the world (Thomas Telford's 1826 structure across the Menai Strait to Anglesey preceded him). It was completed in 1864, with a road suspended from chains which are wedged 21m/70ft into the cliffs. Brunel was designing in the age of horse-drawn transport; fortunately his proposed wooden floor was replaced with metal plates, and his bridge now carries some 4 million cars a year.

Another icon, the Forth Rail Bridge of 1890, is an example of a cantilever structure. The three great iron towers, 104m/340ft high, were built to carry two rail tracks across the Forth, a distance of 1.5 miles (2.5km).

The Second Severn road bridge, linking England and Wales, opened in 1996. It utilises pre-cast sections of concrete, held together by stressing wires; the main central sections are cable-stayed. The whole is a more rigid structure than the original suspension crossing (1966), which was notoriously subject to high winds.

Innovation in bridge design has been overtaken by footbridges, such as Newcastle's marvellous tilting Gateshead Millennium footbridge (2000), and the notorious wobbly Millennium footbridge across the Thames (reopened in 2002 after extra stabilising).

Lewis and Harris
Western Isles

TOURIST INFORMATION CENTRE
26 CROMWELL STREET
STORNOWAY
ISLE OF LEWIS
HS1 2DD

TEL: 01851 703088

Lewis and Harris are joined by a narrow neck of land but retain strong individual identities. They share a strong Gaelic culture and a traditional observance of the Sabbath, which means that on Sundays the restaurants, shops and petrol stations may be closed.

Lewis, the northern part, has great undulating blanket peat moors scattered with lochs, and a surprising density of population for such an isolated place. Steornabhagh (Stornoway) is the administrative centre, a busy fishing port and the only real town on the island. Good roads lead through the crofting communities that hug the shore, and to the mountainous southwest corner, where the white sands of Uig and Reef compete with green islands to steal the view. On a clear day,

you can see the pointed peaks of St Kilda, some 50 miles (80km) away on the horizon.

Harris, the southern sector, is the most beautiful of the Outer Hebrides, with high mountains and deep-cut bays. The subtle browns, greens and smoky greys of the landscape are reflected in

the island's most famous export, Harris Tweed, a hand-woven wool cloth of high quality made here since the 1840s.

The island has many prehistoric monuments and monoliths, of which the avenue and circle of 13 stones at Calanais (Callanish), dating from about 3000BC, are outstanding. The stones are of the underlying rock of the island, Lewisian gneiss, some 2,900 million years old.

Just up the coast, Dun Carloway Broch is a good example of a stone-built circular Iron Age dwelling. Set back from the beach at Bosta is a reconstructed Iron Age house, which can be compared with the evocative 19th-century Blackhouse at Arnol. At Roghadal (Rodel), St Clements Church dates from c1500, and has some curious sculptures on the stone tower.

The luminous sands and turquoise waters of Tràigh Luskentyre, with views to Taransay island, are well worth seeing.

LEFT: THE SITE OF CALLANISH IS SECOND IN ARCHAEOLOGICAL IMPORTANCE ONLY TO STONEHENGE.

FAR LEFT: THE TRADITIONAL THATCHED STONE COTTAGES OF GEARRANNAN BLACKHOUSE VILLAGE.

ABOVE: THE ROCKY ISLAND OF HARRIS IS FAMOUS FOR THE PRODUCTION AND EXPORT OF TWEED.

Skye
Highland

The Isle of Skye is the largest and best known of the Inner Hebrides. Broadford is the main centre for the south, with access to the steep, magnificently scenic road to Elgol. Portree is a more appealing township, and centre for the north of the island. On Skye, the road signs appear in Gaelic as well as in English, an immediate indication that the culture and traditions here are very different from those on the mainland. Skye retains its strong Gaelic identity, and this is encouraged at the college, Sabhal Mor Ostaig, in Sleat, but the economic necessity of generations of emigration have forced the island to become outward-looking.

The romantic and well-loved melody the 'Skye Boat Song' recalls the flight of Charles Edward Stewart (Bonnie Prince Charlie) after his defeat at Culloden in 1746, when the prince was smuggled to Skye from South Uist by Flora Macdonald. He continued his journey in safety to Raasay and then France.

CUILLINS
Every view of the Isle of Skye is dominated by the Cuillins (pronounced 'Coolins'), which reach their peak in the far south with Sgùrr Alasdair (3,309ft/1,009m). The southern mountains are the Black Cuillins, distinct from the lower Red Cuillins.

LEFT: THE CUILLINS, SEEN HERE FROM SLIGACHAN, PROVIDE A DRAMATIC BACKDROP TO MOST VIEWS IN SKYE.

TOURIST INFORMATION CENTRE

BAYFIELD HOUSE
BAYFIELD ROAD
PORTREE
ISLE OF SKYE
IV51 9EL

TEL: 01478 612137

PORTREE

The harbour town of Portree on the eastern coast is the capital of the island, and the centre of island life. The town was named after a royal visit in 1540 by James V – *port righ* means 'king's harbour' – and its formal square is a miniature delight.

DUNVEGAN CASTLE

The MacLeod clan have owned and fought over Skye for many generations. Their home, Dunvegan Castle, is a fortress built on a high rock that was once completely surrounded by the sea, and has been occupied since the 13th century. The most poignant of its treasures is the faded and tattered talisman of the Fairy Flag, a gift to an early clan chief from his fairy lover, with potent powers to rescue the clan at times of peril. The flag has been used twice to turn the course of battle successfully.

TROTTERNISH

Trotternish is the peninsula that sticks up at the northern tip of Skye. Ancient flows of lava have produced sheer cliffs, with shearings and pinnacles down the spine created where softer rocks buckled under the weight of the lava. The most famous is the Old Man of Storr, a black obelisk 160 ft (49m) high.

Mull and Iona
Argyll & Bute

TOURIST INFORMATION CENTRE

THE PIER
CRAIGNURE
ISLE OF MULL
PA65 6AY

TEL: 01680 812377

BELOW, LEFT: THE SHORES OF IONA.

BELOW: IONA ABBEY, BUILT IN THE 13TH CENTURY.

RIGHT: REMOTE DUART CASTLE.

Mull is the largest of the Inner Hebridean islands, covering some 350 square miles (906sq km), with high mountains in the south, and the rugged inlets of Loch Scridain and Loch na Keal in the west. The main settlement is the 19th-century fishing port of Tobermory, in the northeast. The remoteness of the western seaboard makes it ideal habitat for the re-introduced white-tailed eagle, and for golden eagles, buzzards, peregrines and seabirds. To see birds of prey up close, visit Wings Over Mull, a conservation centre at Craignure.

Just a short ride away on the narrow-gauge railway, Torosay Castle is a stately home of 1858, with 12 acres (5ha) of Italianate gardens. On the point of Duart Bay stands a much older edifice, Duart Castle, 13th-century home of the Macleans. West of Ben More, Mull's highest mountain, is the Ardmeanach peninsula, the tip of which is reached via an arduous 5.5-mile (9km) path. Its main sight is a fossilized tree, 12m (40ft) high and up to 50 million years old.

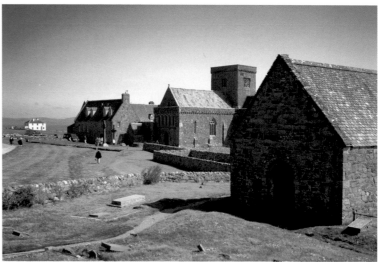

Fionnphort is the access point for Iona, a magical island known since the 6th century as the cradle of Christianity in Scotland. Most visitors make straight for the abbey, but spare time for the remains of the 13th-century priory, built for Augustinian nuns. The Celtic saint Columba came to Iona in AD563 from Ireland, where he was born and educated, and founded his monastery. From it the light of Christianity radiated throughout Europe. Now home to the Iona Community, the abbey welcomes pilgrims from around the world. Beside it is the ancient burial ground of Scottish kings, including Duncan and Macbeth. Excursions take in the island of Staffa, with its hexagonal basalt columns, and Fingal's Cave.

Inverewe Garden

Highland

5 miles (8km) northeast of Gairloch

LEFT AND BELOW: THE NORTH ATLANTIC DRIFT ENCOURAGES THE GROWTH OF INVEREWE'S TROPICAL PLANTS.

POOLEWE
ACHNASHEEN
IV22 2LG

TEL: 01445 781200

In 1862 Osgood Mackenzie (1842–1922) acquired the sporting estate of Inverewe, and on this barren, rocky, salt-wind-blown promontory started to plant shelter belts of trees. Soil and fertilizing seaweed had to be imported by the back-breaking creel-load.

Mackenzie had to wait for two decades before the trees were sufficiently established for him to begin serious planting. He set to work to collect 'every rare exotic tree and shrub which I hear succeeds in Devon, Cornwall, and the west of Ireland.' Like these places, Inverewe benefits from the warmth of the Gulf Stream. Mackenzie's daughter Mairi Sawyer took over the garden on her father's death, and in 1953 it was passed on to the National Trust for Scotland.

Entry to the 50-acre (20ha) garden is through the visitor centre and shop, leading past the south-facing walled garden and through the rock garden. A network of paths leads on through the various walks. The planting is varied and exotic, with something flowering at almost any time of the year and tropical plants bloom here, apparently effortlessly.

Glen Coe

Highland

East of Ballachulish

Whether your first approach to Glen Coe is down from the wide, watery wasteland of Rannoch Moor, or up from the finger of sea that is Loch Leven, you cannot fail to be impressed by the majesty of this long, steep-sided valley. On a clear day it is possible to see the tops of the Aonach Eagach ridge to the north (3,169ft/966m), with its sweeping sides of loose scree, and the peaks of the great spurs of rock known as the Three Sisters to the south, leading down from Bidean nam Bian (3,766ft/1,148m). At the eastern end the glen is guarded by the massive bulk of Buachaille Etive Mor, the 'Great Shepherd of Etive' (3,343ft/1,019m). On other days the tops are hidden in a smur of rain clouds, the waterfalls become torrents and wind funnels up the glen at a terrific rate.

Memories are long in the Highlands, and there is still a frisson between the Macdonalds and the Campbells which dates back to a February night in 1692. At a time when clan leaders were required to swear loyalty to the monarchs William and Mary, Alastair Macdonald of Glen Coe left the unsavoury task as late as possible. When he missed the deadline by several days, Campbell of Glenlyon was sent to make an example of him. Campbell's men were billeted here for two weeks before turning on their hosts in an act of cold-blooded slaughter which left 38 dead. It was a betrayal which has never been forgotten.

TOURIST INFORMATION CENTRE

BALLACHULISH
PA39 4JR

TEL: 0845 2255121

RIGHT: THE SNOWY
BLACK MOUNT AND
RANNOCH MOOR
PROVIDE A PEACEFUL
WINTER LANDSCAPE.

Culzean Castle and Country Park
South Ayrshire
4 miles (6km) west of Maybole

MAYBOLE
KA19 8LE
TEL: 01655 884455

LEFT: ALTHOUGH NOT BUILT FOR DEFENCE, CULZEAN HAS A SUPERB CLIFF-EDGE POSITION.

ABOVE: THE LATE 18TH-CENTURY GATEHOUSE TO CULZEAN CASTLE.

Culzean (pronounced 'Cullane') is a fine 18th-century mansion by master architect Robert Adam, located in an outstanding coastal setting. It is Scotland's most popular National Trust property, partly thanks to the surrounding country park – 563 lush green acres (228ha) of wild gardens and leafy woodland riddled with trails. There is a walled garden, an aviary, a deer park and lots of follies dotted around.

The golden stone castle, romantically set right at the edge of the cliffs, is handsome rather than beautiful, with its baronial towers and castellated roofline. It is reached via a bridge, and rises high above a terraced garden. Inside, it is an 18th-century

show home, the most outstanding achievement of Scottish architect Robert Adam; he worked on it from 1777 to 1792 for the powerful Kennedy family, who had dominated this part of Ayrshire since the 12th century.

Highlights include the graceful oval staircase and the Circular Saloon. The top floor was granted to General Eisenhower in 1945, for his lifetime, as a thanks from the people of Scotland for American help during World War II; there are photographs and mementoes of his visits.

There are spectacular sea views to the craggy island of Ailsa Craig from the Circular Saloon.

Burns National Heritage Park
South Ayrshire
2 miles (3km) south of Ayr

MURDOCH'S LONE
KA7 4PQ
TEL: 01292 443700

BELOW: THE BURNS MONUMENT STANDS IN GROUNDS OVERLOOKING THE RIVER DOON.

Robert 'Rabbie' Burns (1759–96) is Scotland's most famous poet and songwriter, his birthday (25 January) celebrated the world over. He was born into poverty in a tiny cottage in Alloway. With the neighbouring museum and several buildings in the park opposite, it is the main focus of the Heritage Park.

Burns's writings ranged from shrewd and witty observations about the life around him to the deeply romantic and the downright bawdy. Songs like 'A Red, Red Rose' and 'Auld Lang Syne' are an integral thread in the weave of Scottish culture.

BURNS MONUMENT
The Burns 'cult' sprang up quickly after his death, with public subscription finding the money to lay the first stones of the Burns Monument in 1820. That structure is a centre for events celebrating his life and work, and there are great views over his beloved Alloway from the roof. The Heritage Park also offers an audiovisual presentation at the Tam o'Shanter Experience, and the handsome stone bridge that featured in his poetry, the Auld Brig o'Doon, is here, too.

STATUE HOUSE
'Tam o'Shanter' is a rollicking ballad that tells the story of drunken Tam, making his way home one night on his grey mare, and spying on a party of witches. They spot him and chase him, and the mare loses its tail in the flight.

Self-taught sculptor James Thom created a set of vivid statues which bring the characters of the ballad to life. These are now on display in the Statue House.

Loch Lomond and Trossachs National Park
Argyll & Bute
18 miles (29km) north of Glasgow

The romantic beauty of the Highland landscape, epitomized by this accessible and scenic area, was first 'discovered' in the late 18th century. Novelist and poet Sir Walter Scott did much to bring it to the popular eye, with his thrilling poem 'The Lady of the Lake' (1810) set in identifiable locations across the Trossachs, ending at Loch Katrine. Today the national park stretches from the Argyll Forest Park in the west across to Callander, and from Killin in the north to Balloch in the south, just 18 miles (29km) from Glasgow.

This is favourite hiking country, with plenty of waymarked trails and a lovely stretch of the West Highland Way long distance path, which runs down the eastern shore of Loch Lomond. Some 24 miles (38.5km) long, the loch is a playground for watersports dotted with 38 islands. It narrows to the north, where the mountains become bigger and bleaker. Ben Lomond,

on the eastern shore, is a popular 'Munro' hill climb at 3,192ft (973m). Luss, off the A82, is the prettiest village to explore. The Loch Lomond Shores Visitor Centre explains the geology and history of the region.

The Trossachs is the area to the east of Loch Lomond, including the wooded hills of the Queen Elizabeth Forest Park, and the peak of Ben Venue (2,391ft/729m).

Some of the best scenery is around Loch Katrine, with easy walking and a steamboat ride among tree-clad islands.

LEFT: BEN LOMOND
RISES IN THE DISTANCE
BEYOND THE SHORES OF
LOCH LOMOND.

NATIONAL PARK
    GATEWAY CENTRE

LOCH LOMOND
    SHORES
BEN LOMOND WAY
BALLOCH
G83 8QL
TEL: 01389 722199

FAR LEFT, ABOVE: THE
SUN SETS ON A VIEW
OF LOCH LOMOND,
LOOKING TOWARDS THE
ARROCHAR ALPS.

FAR LEFT, BELOW:
A COTTAGE IN LUSS,
A CONSERVATION
VILLAGE ON THE SHORES
OF THE LOCH.

Glasgow

City of Glasgow

41 miles (65km) west of Edinburgh

GLASGOW TOURIST
  INFORMATION CENTRE

11 GEORGE SQUARE
GLASGOW
G2 1DY

TEL: 0141 204 4400

BELOW: CITY CHAMBERS
IN GEORGE SQUARE.
RIGHT: GLASGOW
CATHEDRAL.
FAR RIGHT: GLASGOW'S
COAT-OF-ARMS.

Once Scotland's industrial powerhouse, with its roots in ironworks and shipbuilding, Glasgow has rediscovered its artistic side in recent years. It was European City of Culture in 1990, then City of Architecture and Design in 1999. It is now, arguably, a more exciting place than Edinburgh.

Trade and religion have shaped Glasgow. St Kentigern (AD518–603) is said to have built Glasgow's first church, where the cathedral now stands. The settlement became a royal burgh in 1611 and the Protestant Revolution later that century allowed commerce to flourish. As a port on the west coast, Glasgow was

perfectly located for trade with the English colonies in America, importing tobacco, cotton and rum. The Industrial Revolution helped Glasgow become the workshop of the western world. Money flowed in as ships built on the Clyde flowed out. The city is now adapting to post-industrial life, with an emphasis today on culture and entertainment.

BURRELL COLLECTION

This priceless collection of 9,000 pieces of art from around the world was given to Glasgow in 1944 by Sir William Burrell (1861–1958) and is now housed in the Pollok Country Park. You'll find August Rodin's *The Thinker* in the courtyard. Intriguing old stone doorways lead into different parts of the museum.

GALLERY OF MODERN ART (GOMA)

Check out Peter Howson's painting 'Patriots' (1991), with three loutish men and their snarling bulldogs, as well as huge striped canvases by pop-artist Bridget Riley (born 1931) and works by Andy Warhol (1927–87) and David Hockney (born 1937). Changing exhibitions fill the top floor galleries.

GLASGOW SCIENCE CENTRE

The main attraction at the Science Centre is the Science Mall, with four floors of 500 interactive exhibits. Highlights include distorting mirrors, seeing how an artificial arm picks up signals from your body, and a walk-on piano for those under seven.

HUNTERIAN MUSEUM AND ART GALLERY

William Hunter (1718–83) was a Glasgow-trained physician who left his scientific collections – including anatomical specimens used in teaching – to his old university. The magnificent art collection, in a separate building, originates from Hunter's own purchases of 17th-century Flemish, Dutch and Italian masters.

RENNIE MACKINTOSH TRAIL

The architecture of Charles Rennie Mackintosh (1868–1928) is a distinctive fusion of the flowing lines of Art Nouveau with the simplicity of the Arts and Crafts movement. Mackintosh left his mark on Glasgow, with principal points of interest – the Glasgow School of Art, The Willow Tearooms and the House for an Art Lover – forming the Rennie Mackintosh Trail.

New Lanark
South Lanarkshire
1 mile (1.5km) south of Lanark

BELOW, LEFT: ONE
OF NEW LANARK'S
ATTRACTIONS IS A
SPECTACULAR SEQUENCE
OF THREE WATERFALLS.

BELOW: THE SPINNING
MILL'S NEW BUILDINGS
WERE RAISED BESIDE THE
ESSENTIAL WATER SUPPLY
OF THE RIVER CLYDE.

NEW LANARK WORLD
HERITAGE SITE

NEW LANARK MILLS
LANARK ML11 9DB

TEL: 01555 661345

Glasgow philanthropist David Dale (1739–1806) first developed a cotton manufacturing plant and settlement in this steep-sided valley in 1786. However, it is his son-in-law, the Welshman Robert Owen (1771–1858), who is most clearly identified with the village, which he purchased in 1799. A benevolent idealist, over the next two decades he established a Utopian society here – a model community with improved conditions for the workers and their families, complete with school (it is claimed, with the first day nursery and playground in

the world), institute for adult education, and co-operative village store. The site was later to declined. However, in 1973 the New Lanark Conservation Trust started to restore the site, with the impressive results seen today.

The workers' houses are lived in once more, though the mill no longer manufactures cotton. The process can be understood through the curious high-tech meets heavy engineering Millennium Experience themed 'dark ride', complete with tableaux and sound effects. There is also a millworker's cottage to explore, as well as Robert Owen's house, the school and the Village Store exhibition. Visitors can even stay here, in the 3-star New Lanark Mill hotel or self-catering cottages. The walk to the three waterfalls that lie upstream is worth doing, particularly after rainfall when they are at their best.

Culross

Fife

7 miles (11km) west of Dunfermline

TOURIST INFORMATION CENTRE

1 HIGH STREET, DUNFERMLINE KY12 7DL

TEL: 01383 720999

BELOW, LEFT: THE TOWN CROSS STANDS IN A COBBLED SQUARE.

BELOW, RIGHT: THE ODDLY-SHAPED 'STUDY' DATES FROM 1610.

A preserved Scottish burgh on the north shore of the River Forth, west of Dunfermline, Culross (pronounced 'Cure-oss') looks like the paintings of very old Scottish burghs, all winding, cobbled streets and crow-stepped gables. It had an early involvement in coal-mining and salt panning, mostly through George Bruce, the town's 16th-century entrepreneur. As the local coal was gradually worked out, the emphasis on industrial activity swung to other parts of the Forth Valley and Culross became a backwater, overlooked on the muddy estuary shores.

Many of the substantial 17th- and 18th-century merchants' and workers' houses were never replaced by later, more modern buildings. Paradoxically, it was Culross's poverty that created the picturesque groupings so admired today.

In the 1930s the National Trust for Scotland started buying up properties, which were by that time approaching dereliction. Decades later, many of the houses, fully restored, are now lived in by ordinary people.

Traquair
Borders
1 mile (1.5km) south of Innerleithen

BELOW: TRAQUAIR,
THE OLDEST INHABITED
HOUSE IN SCOTLAND,
IS COMFORTABLE RATHER
THAN GRAND.

TRAQUAIR HOUSE
INNERLEITHEN
EH44 6PW
TEL: 01896 830323

A wonderful air of romance and ancient secrecy surrounds Traquair, a beautiful old castle buried away in the trees 6 miles (9.7km) southeast of Peebles. Traquair House started out as a royal hunting lodge in the 15th century, at the time of the Scottish King James III. The castle's so-called 'modern' extensions were made way back in 1680, and today it presents a serene face to visitors.

Once the Tweed ran so close to the castle that the laird could fish from his windows. That changed in the 17th century, when the river was re-routed by Sir William Stuart, who in 1566 built most of what we see now, in 1566.

Part of Traquair's sense of mystery comes from its connections with the doomed Stewart cause: Mary, Queen of Scots stayed here in 1566 (her bed is now in the King's Room), and the famous Bear Gates have not been opened since 1745, when 'Bonnie Prince Charlie' last rode through. There are secret stairs to the hidden Priest's Room, and touching relics of a time when Catholics were persecuted in Scotland.

An impressive modern venture has been the revival of a brewery at Traquair. Re-established in 1965, it has proved highly successful, and now produces three rich, dark ales for export worldwide – samples are available in the brewery shop.

Stirling
Stirlingshire
21 miles (34km) northeast of Glasgow

HISTORIC SCOTLAND

THE CASTLE
STIRLING FK8 1EJ

TEL: 01786 450000

Stirling Castle's strategic position high on a rocky outcrop, commanding the narrow waist of land between the Forth estuary and the marshlands of the west (now drained), has given it a prominent role in Scottish history. The castle served as a royal palace and was remodelled many times. The ill-fated Mary, Queen of Scots, spent her childhood here and was crowned in the Chapel Royal in 1543.

The town behind and below the castle has other interesting buildings, and was of particular importance in the wars of independence, fought against England in the 13th and 14th centuries. Notable Scottish victories include Stirling Bridge (1297), fought at the Old Bridge just north of the town centre, when William Wallace cleverly split the opposing army in two, and Bannockburn (1314), when Robert the Bruce took charge. Both men are commemorated as local heroes, Wallace with the 220ft (67m) tower, the National Wallace Monument, on the nearby hill of Abbey Craig, and Bruce with a heritage centre on the field of Bannockburn, below the castle.

LEFT: STIRLING CASTLE, KNOWN AS 'THE KEY TO SCOTLAND', ENJOYS A STRATEGIC POSITION ON TOP OF A ROCK.

ABOVE: THE CLIMB TO THE TOP OF THE WALLACE MONUMENT IS REWARDED WITH PANORAMIC VIEWS.

Culloden

Highland

4 miles (6km) east of Inverness

The Jacobite defeat at the Battle of Culloden, fought on 16 April 1746, was the dismal outcome of a civil war that had split families as well as hastening the end of the already disintegrating clan system in Scotland.

Prince Charles Edward Stuart (1720–88), nicknamed Bonnie Prince Charlie, was raised in European exile, the heir to the Scottish throne which the Catholic Stuarts still claimed through James, the Old Pretender (*jacobus* in Latin, hence Jacobite as the name for the political movement). The French were keen on stirring up political matters with the Protestant Hanoverian government in Britain, and encouraged the Prince's madcap expedition to claim the throne in 1745.

Charles landed at Glenfinnan and raised a mixed bag of Highland fighters, some of them coerced by their chiefs. Initially the Prince's army was successful, and reached Derby in northern England before running out of steam. The Highlanders retreated northwards, but by the spring of 1746 the Hanoverian forces were closing in.

When the two armies met at Culloden, the Prince's outnumbered and exhausted forces faced an army of regular soldiers. A tactical blunder placed his Highlanders within range of the government artillery, and the Jacobites were blown away in under an hour. More than 1,200 Jacobites and 400 Hanoverians died in the skirmish. Stones and flags mark the battlefield today, to show where individual clans fell.

In the aftermath, the government leader the Duke of Cumberland earned the title of 'Butcher' when he sanctioned one of the worst atrocities ever carried out by the British Army. Military looting was legalised throughout the Highlands, irrespective of loyalties, and the Highland way of life changed for ever. Jacobite propaganda retreated into sentimentality, and the romantic figure of the Prince in hiding, never betrayed as he fled to exile, became legendary.

ABOVE: A FLAG SHOWS WHERE THE JACOBITES FACED GOVERNMENT (HANOVERIAN) FORCES ON CULLODEN MOOR.

LEFT: THE BATTLE IS COMMEMORATED BY THIS MEMORIAL CAIRN.

CULLODEN VISITOR CENTRE

CULLODEN MOOR INVERNESS IV2 5EU

TEL: 01463 790607

Cairngorms
Highland

BELOW, LEFT: THE
CAIRNGORMS CHAIRLIFT.
BELOW, RIGHT: VIEWS
ACROSS LOCH MORLICH.

TOURIST INFORMATION CENTRE
GRAMPIAN ROAD
AVIEMORE PH22 1PP
TEL: 01479 810363

The highest massif in Britain, with alpine flora and rare wildlife, attracts walkers, rock climbers and skiers. The Cairngorm mountains lie between Speyside and Bracmar, dominated by the four peaks of Ben Macdhui, Braeriach, Cairn Toul and Cairn Gorm. Between them runs the ancient north–south pass of the Lairig Ghru, and around the northwest edge the settlements of Speyside and the resort of Aviemore. The remoteness of the Cairngorms has left them the haunt of golden eagles, ptarmigan, capercaillie and other species that thrive in the deserted corries amid unusual alpine flora. The area was designated Scotland's second national park in 2003.

The once-sleepy railway station of Aviemore was developed in the 1960s as a ski centre, and has little to recommend it unless you are part of the ski scene.

The Rothiemurchus Estate, 1.5 miles (2.5km) to the south, offers a variety of outdoor pursuits in a beautiful setting of mountains, lochs and Caledonian pine forest.

Aviemore is linked by the preserved Strathspey Steam Railway to Boat of Garten. The Royal Society for the Protection of Birds (RSPB) has a visitor centre here. A funicular railway in the Cairngorm ski area east of Aviemore takes visitors up the flank of Cairn Gorm itself.

Dunkeld
Perth & Kinross
10 miles (16km) west of Blairgowrie

With the exception of the diminutive 13th-century cathedral, the original settlement of Dunkeld was destroyed by the Jacobites after their victory at Killiecrankie in 1689. It was rebuilt, with terraced houses packed into a compact centre of just two main streets: Cathedral Street and High Street, with a neat little square, the Cross. Many of the houses are whitewashed, and its pleasing uniformity owes much to restoration by the National Trust for Scotland.

By the partly restored cathedral stands the 'Parent Larch', a tree imported from Austria in 1738 and the source of many of the trees in the surrounding forests, planted between 1738 and 1830 by the Dukes of Atholl. A walk beside the River Braan leads past the tallest Douglas fir in Britain (211ft/64.3m) to the Hermitage, an 18th-century folly. The celebrated 18th-century fiddler Neil Gow was born across the river, and his grave is at Little Dunkeld.

To the east, the Loch of the Lowes is in the care of the Scottish Wildlife Trust and is noted for breeding ospreys.

LEFT AND ABOVE:
DUNKELD IS AT THE
CENTRE OF A NETWORK
OF RIVERSIDE AND
WOODLAND WALKS.

TOURIST INFORMATION
CENTRE

THE CROSS
DUNKELD
PH8 0AN

TEL: 01350 727688

From beside one of the houses restored under the Trust's 'Little Houses Scheme', the Ell House, a lane leads right to the cathedral, invisible from most of the town. Beautifully situated beside the River Tay, the building of the cathedral dates mostly from the 14th and 15th centuries. The nave and aisles have been roofless since 1560, but the choir is now the parish church. An exhibition on display in the Chapter House outlines the history of both town and cathedral.

ABOVE: A DETAIL FROM
A GRAVESTONE CARVING
IN THE CHURCHYARD OF
DUNKELD CATHEDRAL.

LEFT: THE VILLAGE OF
DUNKELD IS DOMINATED
BY THE TOWER OF ITS
MEDIEVAL CATHEDRAL.

Blair Castle
Perth & Kinross
8 miles (13km) north of Pitlochry

This turreted mansion, set against a background of dark green forestry, seems the archetypal romantic Scottish castle, admired on shortbread tins the world over. It has been the ancestral home of the Murray and Stewart Dukes and Earls of Atholl for over 700 years, and to this day has its own private army, the Atholl Highlanders, thanks to a favour granted by Queen Victoria in 1845.

The medieval castle occupied a strategic position on the main route to Inverness, so it's no surprise that in 1652 Cromwell's army seized it. The castle also played a role in the Jacobite risings of 1715 and 1745, when the Murray family's loyalties were tragically divided. In more peaceful times, the castle was recast as a Georgian mansion by the 2nd Duke and, with the coming of the railway in 1863, a Victorian-style remodelling took place, creating the picturesque building seen today.

There is plenty to see in the castle, from portraits and rich furnishings to an original copy of the National Covenant and the small tartan-clad tower room where Bonnie Prince Charlie slept in 1745. Look for Raeburn's portrait of the legendary fiddler and composer Neil Gow (1727–1807), and Gow's own fiddle, on display in the ballroom. The mature gardens and grounds – including Diana's Grove, with conifers up to 188ft (59m) high – are also worth exploring.

LEFT: BLAIR CASTLE, BUILT FOR THE ATHOLL FAMILY IN 1269, WAS ORIGINALLY KNOWN AS COMYN'S TOWER.

BLAIR CASTLE

BLAIR ATHOLL
PITLOCHRY
PH18 5TL

TEL: 01796 481207

Palace of Holyroodhouse
City of Edinburgh
413 miles (661km) north of London

This pepperpot-towered castle at the foot of the Royal Mile is the Queen's official residence in Scotland, which means it may be closed for odd days at short notice to make way for investitures, royal garden parties and other state occasions. The Palace of Holyroodhouse offers all the advantages of exploring a living palace steeped with history and filled with works of art belonging to the Royal Collection. More precious artworks are on view in the stunning new Queen's Gallery by the entrance and opposite the new Scottish Parliament Building; there is also a well-stocked gift shop here.

The palace was probably founded in 1128 as an Augustinian monastery. In the 15th century it became a guesthouse for the neighbouring Holyrood Abbey (now a scenic ruin), and its name is said to derive from the Holy Rood, a fragment of Christ's cross belonging to David I (c1080–1153). Mary, Queen of Scots stayed here, and a brass plate marks where her favourite, David Rizzio was murdered in her private apartments in the west tower in 1566. After serious fire damage in 1650 during the Civil War, major rebuilding was required. Bonnie Prince Charlie held court here in 1745, followed by George IV on his triumphant visit to the city in 1822, and later Queen Victoria on her way to Balmoral. The state rooms, designed for Charles II by architect William Bruce (1630–1710) and hung with Brussels tapestries, are particularly elaborate and splendid.

PALACE OF
   HOLYROODHOUSE
EDINBURGH EH4 1DX
TEL: 0131 556 5100

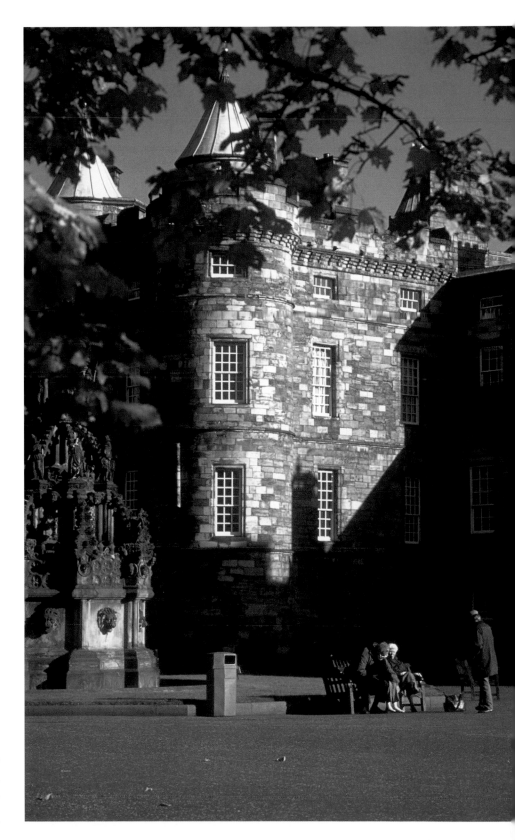

RIGHT: THE PALACE OF HOLYROODHOUSE IS STEEPED IN A HISTORY OF DARK DEEDS.

Edinburgh Castle
City of Edinburgh

Edinburgh Castle towers over the city from its perch high on a wedge of volcanic rock, a solid symbol of the Scottish nation which has withstood centuries of battering. It owes its defensive position to a volcano, which became extinct 70 million years ago. The volcanic rock withstood the Ice Age glaciers, which scoured the landscape around it, creating near-vertical faces to the north and south and leaving a descending 'tail' of rock to the east – the ridge occupied today by the Royal Mile.

Bronze Age people settled on the top around 850BC, and in AD600 it was occupied by an army who called it 'Din Eidyn'. By the Middle Ages it was a heavily fortified site and royal residence.

A key event in the castle's history was the 'Lang (long) Seige' of 1567–73, by James VI's regent. James had been born in the castle in 1566, and it was occupied by supporters of his mother, Mary, Queen of Scots. They held out for two years against the forces of regent James Douglas, Earl of Morton (c1516–81) and his English back-up. Much of the castle was destroyed, and it was the victorious Morton who instigated the rebuilding.

Later royalty preferred the comforts of Holyroodhouse, and Oliver Cromwell's army converted the 16th-century Great Hall into a barracks for his soldiers when he took the castle in 1650 (since restored, its hammerbeam roof is notable). The castle's primary function has been as a garrison fortress ever since.

EDINBURGH CASTLE
CASTLE HILL
EDINBURGH EH1 2NG
TEL: 0131 225 9846

RIGHT: THE ESPLANADE, EDINBURGH CASTLE. IN SUMMER; THIS AREA IS THE SETTING FOR THE MILITARY TATTOO.

ARGYLE BATTERY

This great terrace offers views north over the city. Behind are the Lang Stairs — a steep, curved flight of steps, which provided the main entrance in medieval times.

ST MARGARET'S CHAPEL

The oldest structure in the castle is the 12th-century chapel, dedicated to St Margaret by her son, King David I. Margaret was the wife of Malcolm III and died here in 1093. On the rampart outside is a huge cannon, Mons Meg, a gift in 1457 to James II.

SCOTTISH NATIONAL WAR MEMORIAL

The National War Memorial was designed by Sir Robert Lorimer in 1923–28 to honour the Scottish personnel who died in the two World Wars.

CROWN ROOM

In the Crown Room are kept the ancient Honours of Scotland, consisting of crown, sceptre and sword. The crown dates from 1540, and is made of Scottish gold, studded with semi-precious stones from the Cairngorms.

Royal Botanic Garden
City of Edinburgh

The Botanics, as it is known locally, boasts 15,500 plant species on display, lending weight to its claim to be one of the largest collections of living plants in the world. This total includes some 5,000 species in the rock garden alone (seen to best advantage in May). Occupying this site since 1823, it covers over 70 acres (28ha) of beautifully landscaped and wooded grounds to the north of the city centre, forming a minutely maintained green oasis.

There are ten greenhouses alone to explore, collectively called the Glasshouse Experience and offering the perfect escape on chilly days. They include an amazingly tall palm house

ABOVE: GIANT WATER-LILIES ARE FEATURED HIGHLIGHTS IN THE AQUATIC HOUSE.

dating back to 1858, and the Tropical Aquatic House, where there is an above-the-waterline view of giant waterlilies, followed – downstairs – by an underwater view of fish swimming through the roots.

Outdoors, the plants of the Chinese Hillside and the Heath Garden are particularly interesting, and in summer the herbaceous border, backed by a tall beech hedge, is breathtaking. This is a great place for a break, and for children to let off steam and feed the inquisitive grey squirrels.

Exhibitions of contemporary art and photography are held in the different buildings around the site.

LEFT: A SECLUDED CORNER OF THE OASIS THAT IS THE ROYAL BOTANIC GARDEN.

20A INVERLIETH ROW
EDINBURGH EH3 5LR

TEL: 0131 552 7171

Dundee

City of Dundee
18 miles (29km) northeast of Perth

Dundee was founded on a 19th-century industrial base which was famously reduced to the three 'Js': jam, jute and journalism. Today it sprawls untidily along the northern shore of the Firth of Tay. Speed past on the ring road, however, and you'll miss a treat, for Dundee's waterfront has undergone a transformation. The focus is Discovery Point, centring on a famous heroine of polar exploration, the three-masted Royal Research Ship *Discovery*, which was built here in 1900–01. The story of her planning and construction is told in the museum alongside, with models, audio clips and objects that bring the city's ship-building to life. *Discovery*'s maiden voyage, under the command of a young Robert Falcon Scott (1868–1912), was to Antarctica, where in 1902 she became frozen in the pack ice. She was to remain there for two long winters, while scientific research was undertaken and Scott made an unsuccessful attempt to reach the South Pole. It's a fascinating story, and to see the cramped quarters and realize the scale of the supplies needed for such an expedition makes the tour of the ship all the more interesting.

ABOVE: THE PRIDE OF PANMUIR YARD, WHERE SHE WAS BUILT, *DISCOVERY* IS NOW A MAJOR TOURIST ATTRACTION AT HER BIRTHPLACE.

TOURIST INFORMATION CENTRE

21 CASTLE STREET
DUNDEE DD1 3AA
TEL: 01382 527527

East Neuk
Fife

MUSEUM AND HERITAGE
CENTRE

62–64 MARKETGATE
CRAIL KY10 3TL

TEL: 01333 450869

TOURIST INFORMATION CENTRE

SCOTTISH FISHERIES MUSEUM
EAST SHORE
ANSTRUTHER KY10 3AB

TEL: 01333 311073

Neuk is the Scottish word for corner, and the East Neuk is the name given to eastern Fife. Today it has a prosperous, well-farmed look, with rich grainfields beyond the hedgerows, but in the 15th century James II of Scotland referred to its poverty with the description, a 'beggar's mantle, fringed with gold'. The East Neuk is noted for its charming old fishing villages.

CRAIL

The most easterly of the villages, Crail has a charter dating back to 1178 and a much-photographed 16th-century harbour. Former trading links with the Low Countries show up in the architecture, characterized by pantile roofs and high, stepped gables. The square-towered tolbooth even has a Dutch bell, cast in 1520. In nearby Marketgate there are some fine 17th- and 18th-century townhouses and a mercat (market) cross.

ANSTRUTHER

Next west is Anstruther, a larger resort town and former herring port, where seafront shops sell fish and chips and colourful beach toys. The Scottish Fisheries Museum is housed in historic waterfront buildings around a central courtyard, and illustrates the past and present life of Scottish fishermen and their families. The town also has a history of smuggling, which centred on the Dreel *burn* (stream) and the 16th-century Smuggler's Inn.

PITTENWEEM

Further west again is Pittenweem, the main fisheries port for
the East Neuk. The town dates back to the 7th century, when
St Fillan based himself in a cave here (in Cove Wynd) while
converting the local Picts to Christianity. A priory grew up
here in the 13th century, and the harbour dates from the 16th
century. Artists are particularly attracted to the town, and there
are plenty of small galleries to explore.

ST MONANS AND ELIE

The tiny houses of the next village, St Monan's, crowd around its
harbour, where ship-building as well as fish brought prosperity in
the 19th century. The squat Auld Kirk (old church) standing alone
at the western end dates from 1362. Elie is the most westerly of
the East Neuk villages, and its golden sands made it a popular
holiday resort in the late 19th century. A causeway leads to a
rocky islet, with panoramic views and a busy watersports centre.

Crathes Castle

Aberdeenshire

3 miles (5km) east of Banchory

TOURIST INFORMATION CENTRE

BRIDGE STREET
BANCHORY AB31 5QJ

TEL: 01330 822000

BELOW: CRATHES CASTLE, VIEWED FROM THE COLOURFUL HERBACEOUS BORDERS OF THE LOWER GARDEN.

In 1323 Robert the Bruce gifted a parcel of land, east of Banchory, to Alexander Burnard (Burnett) of Leys, presenting him with a carved and bejewelled ivory horn as a symbol of tenure. In 1553 a castle was started on the site, which took almost 50 years to complete. It is now a delightful example of a Baronial-style tower-house, and is famous for its Jacobean ceilings, boldly painted with figures, designs and mottoes. While the interior of the castle presents the comfortable setting of mellow furnishings, oak-carved panels and family portraits you might expect, it is the 3.75-acre (1.5ha) walled garden glimpsed from the windows which steals the show.

Massive hedges of Irish yew, planted up to 300 years ago, and carved into undulating 'egg and cup' topiary sculptures, dominate the upper garden. They frame and shelter themed 'rooms', helping to create a micro-climate in which a rich variety of plants thrive. The deep herbaceous borders of the lower garden are breathtaking in the colour and variety of their planting, with the June border linking the vistas of the castle and a venerable doocote (dovecote). In their present form, these remarkable gardens reflect a labour of love by Sir James and Lady Sybil Burnett in the early 20th century, and their work is continued by the National Trust for Scotland.

St Andrews

Fife

9 miles (14km) east of Cupar

This attractive, breezy town is set on the east coast, with a sandy bay to the north, and a narrow harbour to the south. Before the Reformation it was the ecclesiastical and scholarly centre of Scotland, and it has the country's oldest university, founded in 1413. It is also the home of the Royal and Ancient Golf Club, founded in 1754 and still the ruling authority on the game worldwide.

The town received its royal charter in 1140, and the cathedral was started 20 years later. After Protestant reformer John Knox preached here in 1559, it was smashed up, and just a century later left derelict. Near the gaunt ruins of the cathedral stand the remains of the 12th-century St Rule's Church.

LEFT AND ABOVE: THE RUINED REMAINS OF ST ANDREWS CATHEDRAL, FOUNDED IN THE 12TH CENTURY.

TOURIST INFORMATION CENTRE
70 MARKET STREET
ST ANDREWS KY16 9NU
TEL: 01334 472021

Index